TO WALK WITH CHRIST

Praying with the Spiritual Exercises
of Saint Ignatius

Laurence L. Gooley, S.J.

Saint Louis
The Institute of Jesuit Sources

D0877436

Number 21 in Series IV:
Studies on Jesuit Topics

©1998, The Institute of Jesuit Sources
3700 West Pine Boulevard
Saint Louis, MO, 63108
TEL: 314-977-7257
FAX: 314-977-7263
e-mail: IJS@SLU.EDU

Library of Congress Card Number 98-71693
ISBN 1-880810-33-6

This book is a revised version of *A Pilgrimage: Praying with the Spiritual Exercises of St. Ignatius*, privately published by the author in 1993 and revised by him in 1996 and again in 1997.

TABLE OF CONTENTS

FOREWORD

PRAYING WITH THE SPIRITUAL EXERCISES

The Process:
This book on the Exercises has been written for Christian Life Communities to use as a prayer experience during their meetings, but it may be used for the same purpose by any other group or may be used as a help for individuals when making the Exercises as a retreat.

As a Prayer Experience: When going through this book as a "prayer experience," the CLC community moves together through the entire set of exercises, normally not repeating an exercise unless there is a strong desire to do so. A spiritual director is recommended. A member may, at any time, request feedback and guidance from the community.

As a Retreat Experience: This book may also be used by individuals who are making the Exercises as a retreat experience. In this case, the retreatant spends time on any given exercise as long as there is fruit. This, of course, is done under the guidance of the Spirit through a retreat director.

In Christian Life Community, both processes (praying with the Exercises and making them as a retreat) are strongly encouraged.

PREVIEWING THIS HANDBOOK

Before actually beginning, it would be good for you to familiarize yourselves with this handbook in the following ways:

- Thumb through the book to become familiar with its format and contents.

- Familiarize yourself with the *CLC Meeting Format* on pages xi-xii.

- Read the *Structure of the Spiritual Exercises* on page xiv.

- Read *The Process of Praying with the Spiritual Exercises* on page ix.

- Read *Dispositions for Entering into the Exercises* on pages xvi-xvii.

* * * * * * * * * *

Length of Time Used:

It is recommended that this book be completed over the period of about nine months, beginning in the Fall, doing the exercises in accordance with the liturgical year. Communities which meet bi-monthly may do this either by doing two exercises in between meetings or by skipping certain exercises.

CLC Meeting Format

As always, the meeting is to be adapted to the needs of the community.

Personal Dimension:

Check-in:
Briefly say how you are feeling as you begin the meeting.

Opening Prayer:
Using music, scripture, and so on (5 minutes).

Read Aloud the Entire Exercise.

Sharing:
"What moved me in this exercise, and how is it reflected in my life?" Sharings are simply received in silence. The one sharing is free to ask for feedback. After the sharings are finished, members may be asked if there is anything they wish to add.

Break.

Community Dimension:

Open Conversation:
About anything affecting the life of the community, including how God is moving the community through the sharings and spiritual movements of each member.

Next Meeting:

Preview the exercise to be used for the next meeting's sharing.

Business:

Issues, location of next meeting, facilitator. . . .

Review of Evening:

"How was I moved during this meeting? Where did I feel positive energy? Where did I feel discomfort?"

Closing Prayer:

Social.

Purpose of the Spiritual Exercises

The purpose of the Spiritual Exercises has been described in many ways. St. Ignatius says they are intended to help one discover one's true self and to put such order into one's life that all decisions will be made free of any unhealthy attachments. Some interpret this to mean that the Exercises are a process of reformation. Others say they are a school of prayer. Still others say that the Exercises are a process of decision-making. All these are, in some ways, true.

Another and more over-arching way to consider the Spiritual Exercises is as a process of praying the Gospels to become identified with Jesus Christ in loving and serving God in all things. Personal renewal, becoming deepened in prayer, and Spirit-filled decision making are the gifts, the fruits of this experience. The immediate experience is always the direct encounter with God in Jesus Christ.

"Reflections" and "Suggestions" supplement the prayer of each exercise. The Consciousness Examen and Ignatius's inspired rules for discerning one's interior movements are printed among the Appendices in the back of the book to assist in this spiritual pilgrimage of love.

"Whoever has seen me has seen the Father."
—John 14:9

STRUCTURE OF THE SPIRITUAL EXERCISES

The Spiritual Exercises are just what they say: things to do, like spiritual aerobics. They offer a step-by-step process of meditations and contemplations through which people come to discover their true selves, in union with Jesus Christ, in order to love and serve God in all things.

The Spiritual Exercises are divided into four sections which Ignatius calls "weeks" (this book calls them "graces"). These weeks, or graces, are not restricted to seven days each. They are periods of time which vary in length according to the experience and needs of the person making the Exercises.

The First Grace (Week) leads us to gratitude for God's unconditional love for us just as we are. The Second Grace (Week) leads us to intimacy and companionship with Jesus, taking on his heart and mind. The Third Grace (Week) affirms our commitment to follow him unconditionally through uniting our passions and deaths with his, and the Fourth Grace (Week) confirms our union with him in loving and serving God in true spiritual freedom.

The text of the Exercises is the Gospel; and, just as there is no one way to live out the Gospel, so there is no one experience of the Exercises. It will be your own life experiences that you will be looking at. Thus, going through the Spiritual Exercises is not about getting into Ignatius's experience; it is primarily about getting into your own. Each of you will be doing *your own* spiritual exercises.

Believe me, an hour is coming,

and is already here, when authentic worshippers

will worship the Father in spirit and truth.

Indeed, it is just such worshippers

the Father seeks.

God is spirit, and those who worship . . .

must worship in spirit and truth.

—John 4:21-24

DISPOSITIONS FOR ENTERING INTO THE EXERCISES

i. These spiritual exercises are for your inner self, as physical exercises are for your body. They help you discern the true way of living that makes God's love in you possible.

ii. It is helpful to have a spiritual director during these exercises. It is also useful to have a regular prayer period each day.

iii. Pray to enter into these exercises with courage and generosity. Then God will bring you to personal enrichment and use you to bring others to theirs.

iv. Whenever you feel that nothing is happening to you during this time, remain faithful to your prayer, to the suggestions of these exercises, to the suggestions of your spiritual director.

v. It is easy to pray when feeling spiritually consoled. When you feel empty and would like to shorten your prayer, recognize this as temptation and stay in prayer slightly longer than planned. This helps develop the habit of fidelity to God.

vi. If you feel spiritually alive, be cautious about making impulsive promises or plans.

vii. Seek openness and availability to God by being willing to make personal choices different from what you feel inclined to make at this point in your life.

viii. Pay attention not so much to your thoughts as to what you feel and what you are experiencing during these exercises.

(Adapted from the introductory notes, or "Annotations," to the Exercises)

Take, Lord, and receive all my liberty,

my memory, my understanding,

and my entire will.

All I have and call my own

You have given to me.

To you, Lord, I return it.

Everything is yours; do with it what you will.

Give me only your love and your grace;

That is enough for me.

—Saint Ignatius of Loyola

READING THE LIFE OF IGNATIUS

Being familiar with the life of Ignatius of Loyola is very helpful in experiencing and understanding his Spiritual Exercises. As an introduction to the Exercises, read his story on pages 133ff. You may do this in one meeting or over a period of several meetings.

After the reading, share with one another your reaction to it, using the following questions as a guide:

- How did Ignatius's story touch you?

- What moved you in it?

- Do you see any similarities between his life and yours? What are they?

- Any other aspects of his life strike you?

It would be helpful to re-read Ignatius's life from time to time. Different aspects of it may strike you according to where you are in your experience of the Exercises.

PART ONE

THE PRINCIPLE AND FOUNDATION OF THE SPIRITUAL EXERCISES

God who loves us creates us
and wants to share life with us forever.
Our love response takes shape in our praise
and honor and service of the God of our life.
All the things in this world are also created because of God's
love, and they become a context of gifts,
presented to us so that we can know God more easily
and make a return of love more readily.
As a result, we show reverence for all the gifts of creation
and collaborate with God in using them so that, by being
good stewards, we develop as loving persons in our care for
God's world and its development.
But if we abuse any of these gifts of creation or, on the
contrary, take them as the center of our lives,
we break our relationship with God
and hinder our growth as loving persons.
In everyday life, then, we must hold ourselves in a balance
before all created gifts insofar as we have a choice
and are not bound by some responsibility.
We should not fix our desires on health or sickness, wealth
or poverty, success or failure, a long life or a short one.
For everything has the potential of calling forth in us
a more loving response to our life forever with God.
Our only desire and our one choice should be this:
I want and I choose what better leads
to God's deepening life in me.[1]

---

[1] *David L. Fleming, S.J., Draw Me Into Your Friendship: The Spiritual Exercises, A Literal Translation and a Contemporary Reading* (St. Louis: Institute of Jesuit Sources, 1996), p.27.

THE FIRST EXERCISE: THE "PRINCIPLE AND FOUNDATION" OF THE SPIRITUAL EXERCISES

. . . with generous and open hearts . . . .

What will help you most in praying with the Exercises is to enter into them with great courage and generosity. If you offer your will and your freedom, God will be able to make use of who you are and all that you have to accomplish God's desires in you. I find myself invited into the presence of God . . . I feel drawn to give all my attention to prayer.

Grace:

I pray repeatedly for an open and generous heart before God.

Prayer:

  i. Jeremiah 29:11-14. "I know well the plans I have in mind for you." I speak to God, rejoicing because God desires my well-being and not my woe. . . .

 ii. Isaiah 25:1-8. "For you have fulfilled your wonderful plans of old." I speak to God proclaiming what God has done . . . what God is doing . . . what God will do for me.

iii. Isaiah 55:1-5. "Come to me that you may have life." An invitation to come as I am . . . a promise of life . . . a proclamation of what God is already doing for me....

 iv. Psalm 148. "Sing to the Lord a new song." Praise God from the heavens and earth. Praise God for lifting up the people, those close to God, the faithful ones. . . .

Closing:

As I feel moved, I express as a friend to a friend my thanks, praise, and total trust in God, using my body, mind, and spirit.

Reflections:

This exercise is on what Saint Ignatius calls the "Principle and Foundation," which is his vision statement for the whole of the Spiritual Exercises. Placed at the beginning of the Exercises, it states Ignatius's conviction that God creates us out of love and that we are to return that love with full and generous hearts. This is the goal of our lives.

The Principle and Foundation leads us to an inner freedom and openness to the fullness of life that God desires for us. Our work is to be available to this. That is why we pray to be open and generous to God, that the fears and doubts may be removed from our hearts. This grace makes possible the experience of the rest of the Exercises.

Suggestions:

i. Ask in your prayer what the blocks are that keep you from openness and generosity to God.

ii. Prepare for prayer by deciding the night before or early in the morning when and where you will pray.

iii. Use a notebook to jot down any feelings or questions you have in your prayer. Share with your companions.

iv. Share the hopes and fears that each of you brings to this experience. In prayer, bring all of these to God.

v. In your prayer, you need not use all the scripture passages that are given.

Behold God beholding you—and smiling![2]

---

[2] *Anthony de Mello, S.J., cited in Michael Harter, S.J. (ed.), Hearts on Fire* (Saint Louis: Institute of Jesuit Sources, 1993), p. 9.

THE SECOND EXERCISE: THE "PRINCIPLE AND FOUNDATION" (CONTINUED)

Life Is Gift . . . .

I am aware of how much God has given me—my family, the places I grew up, my friends, my education, my adult life. I look around at creation and become aware of all God's gifts. I stand with awe and gratitude at the goodness of God and the love of that God in giving us the many gifts. I see that God's love for us has no limits . . . I find myself invited into the presence of God . . . I give all my attention to prayer.

Grace:

I pray to be overwhelmed by the goodness of God to me.

Prayer:
   i. Genesis 1:1-2:4a. "God looked at everything . . . and found it very good." God looks at me and finds me very good.

   ii. Psalm 8. "When I behold the heavens . . . the moon and the stars . . . what are men and women that you should be mindful of them?" I let God fill me with awe and wonder of God's gift of self to us who dwell on earth . . . .

   iii. Hosea 11:1-5. "I fostered them like one who raises an infant to one's cheeks." I allow this amazing truth to be my experience—God draws me with human cords, with bands of love. . . .

iv. 1 Corinthians 12:4-12. "It is the one and the same Spirit who produces all these gifts." I celebrate the gifts that have been chosen for me. . . .

Closing:

Whenever I feel moved in the course of my prayer and as I reverently conclude this special time, I open my heart to God as a friend to a friend.

Reflections:

This is a continuation of the "Principle and Foundation," the vision statement of the entire Exercises. This exercise relates to the fundamental necessity of a positive vision of life: God is good, the world is good, I am good, all creation is good, even technology. God's creation is not only an outpouring of love; God's love remains present in all. Creation not only occurred in the beginning; it is still occurring today as each new reality emerges.

This truth does not blind us to the reality of evil in our world. This we will pray over later. For the moment, all we are focusing on is the fact that God's love sustains all things.

What we are praying for here is to let the truth of this sink in, to pray to receive the gift of faith so that the truth that all is good will characterize our vision of life and the world. This is an introductory exercise to help dispose us to generosity and openness as we begin *Praying with the Spiritual Exercises.*

Suggestions:

    i. Before beginning, pause for a moment or two to slow down from a busy day. Place your preoccupations aside, even if you have to do this over and over again. If nothing else seems possible, recall how pleased God is with your efforts to pray.

    ii. Quietly read one or all of the scripture passages given above in this exercise, and be aware of how you are feeling. It is these feelings that you bring in to your prayer and that you share with your community.

    iii. Pray together as a community in the light of what you have all shared.

    iv. Again, in your prayer you need not use all the scripture passages that have been given.

THE THIRD EXERCISE: THE "PRINCIPLE AND FOUNDATION" (CONTINUED)

God Loves Me . . . .

I look around me and see a world that is fast changing. It is a far different world from the one my parents lived in, and their parents before them. How did they see God loving and caring for them? How do I see God loving and caring for me? In faith I see that all is intimately connected; God's love is everywhere. All creation in all ages is brought together by this love. I want to experience this and share it with others in all things . . . I find myself in the presence of God . . . I give all my attention to prayer.

Grace:

I ask for what I desire: to experience in the depths of my heart God's love for me.

Prayer:

i. Psalm 139:1-18. "Your right hand shall hold me fast." I am like a child whom God holds like a loving parent. . . .

ii. Matthew 10:26-31. "Every hair of your head has been counted." God is telling me not to be afraid . . . that I am precious . . . that I am worth more than a flock of sparrows . . . .

iii. Luke 15:11-32. "[Your brother] was lost and is found." I know when I become lost that God will come running to me and hold me and kiss me and bring me back home. . . .

iv. John 15:1-17. "As the Father has loved me, so I have loved you." I am in awe at how often Jesus tells me this. Do I still doubt?

Closing:

I converse with God like a close friend or a loving parent, believing that God truly hears me, loves me, and will care for me.

Reflections:

God continually loves us into life. Everything in this world is a gift given to us by God so that we can know God more easily and return that love more readily.

Ignatius sets before us an ideal. We accept the gifts of this life insofar as they help us develop as loving persons; but if any of them become the center and goal of our lives, they displace God and hinder our growth towards God.

As a result, we are to hold ourselves in a kind of balance between having or not having these gifts—even with respect to health or sickness, wealth or poverty, success or failure, a long life or a short one—until we know what God desires for us. We choose whatever leads to the deepening of God's life within us.

This grace of choosing only what God desires for us is the hardest for our culture to receive, for that culture says that we are worthless in ourselves until we have something. The ideal that is this grace is clearly beyond the reach of our own efforts. It is pure gift. We do not achieve this way of living by our own doing. We are invited into it by God.

Ignatius's "Principle and Foundation," in both its personal and social contexts, is something to be prayed for. This grace comes again and again. It is a condition for doing the rest of the Exercises.

Suggestions:

i. Toward the end of your prayer, talk directly to God as a friend talks to a friend about the feelings that surfaced during your prayer. Ask to learn what your feelings are saying to you.

ii. See the Consciousness Examen (page 122f), as a way of reviewing your whole day. Use the Examen in your efforts to be invited into the "Principle and Foundation."

iii. You have seen Ignatius's faith-vision. What is your faith vision, the foundation of your life in God? Pray with this, expressing what is in your heart, whatever it is. Let an image, symbol, story, scripture, song, or word surface for you. Stay with it. Let it speak to you. Now write, draw, sculpt, color, express your personal faith-vision. . . .

Oh, Lord my God,
You called me from the sleep of nothingness
merely because in your tremendous love
you want to make good and beautiful beings.
You have called me by my name in my mother's womb.
You have given me breath and light and movement
and walked with me every moment of my existence.
I am amazed, Lord God of the universe,
that you attend to me and, more, cherish me.
Create in me the faithfulness that moves you,
and I will trust you and yearn for you all my days.[3]

---

[3] Joseph A. Tetlow, S.J., cited in Harter, *op. cit.*, p. 12.

TRANSITION TO THE FIRST GRACE (FIRST
WEEK) OF THE EXERCISES:

*I know that you
can do all things,
and that no purpose of yours
can be hindered.*

*I have dealt with great things
that I do not understand:
things too wonderful for me,
which I cannot know.*

*I had heard of you
by word of mouth,
but now my eye has seen you.
Therefore I disown
what I have said, and
repent
in dust and ashes.*

—Job 42:1-6

PART TWO

THE FIRST GRACE (FIRST WEEK): GOD LOVES ME JUST AS I AM

THE FIRST EXERCISE: THE PRESENCE OF EVIL IN THE WORLD

You are precious in my eyes and glorious and I love you. . .

I always experience confusion when I reflect on the reality of sin in the world. It is hard to sort out what belongs to me and what doesn't. The world is not complete. There is a lot of good, but there is also a lot of evil in it. It is very confusing. What is it that wants to hinder the loving purpose of God? Why does our world continually try to frustrate the loving creative act of God? I see this on TV news and on the city streets . . . I quiet myself and relax in the presence of God . . . I acknowledge that I am completely dependent on God.

The Scene:
I see the reality of evil throughout the world.

Grace:
I ask for what I desire: a deep-felt awareness of my sinfulness and that of the world, so that, feeling sorrow and confusion, I will turn to Christ for help and will rely more constantly on God's forgiving love.

Prayer:

    i. Amos 2:6-8. "They trample the heads of the weak into the dust of the earth, and force the lowly out of the way." I experience this in all creation and in me personally.

    ii. Isaiah 3:13-17. "The loot you wrested from the poor is in your houses." I see greed all around me and within me. I see the crushing of people, the grinding down of the poor, the degradation of women, the abuse of children.

    iii. John 17:23. "You loved them as you loved me." I am aware of my lack of love in . . . .

    iv. Luke 19:41-44. "Jesus wept over the city and said, 'If only you had known the path to peace this day.'" With Jesus I look over the city and over the world in which I live. Jesus weeps; with him I weep. . . .

Closing:

    I see Jesus on the cross. I speak with him as a friend to a friend out of what is in my heart.

Reflections:

    We have been praying for the gift of seeing all creation as an outpouring of God's love. Experiencing this makes us aware at the same time of the reality of evil in the world. The more we experience love, the more we experience the lack of it. Seeing how creation is an outpouring of God's love, even though we also see evil in it, is what the rest of the Spiritual Exercises is about. For now, the work of grace is simply to become more sensitized to the lack of response to God's love in and around us. This is the beginning of the movement into the First Grace (Week).

Part of the deceit of sin is to blind us from seeing it for what it really is—deceit. We see it within ourselves and among nations. More and more of our world culture advertises that everything must be held in an urgent eternal now. It is imbued with a compulsion for satiation and its attendant behaviors of domination, violence, destruction of the environment, and blindness to the needs of the elderly and the poor, especially women and children.

This is true even of the American church. It has often become so inculturated into the American ethos of unrestrained consumerism that the Church has lost much of its power to believe or act for justice in society. Anything that diminishes the vision and power of the Gospel is the fruit of a dark spirit and is contrary to living in the freedom of God. The grace of the first week is to see this, within the all-encompassing love of God.[1]

Suggestions:

i. Where do you see the work of evil in you and around you?

ii. Let your prayer and your day carry over into each other.

iii. Read *Making Moral Choices—Discernment of Spirits During the First Grace (Week)* on pages 124ff.

---

[1] See Walter Brueggemann, *The Prophetic Imagination* (Philadelphia: Fortress Press, 1983), p. 11.

THE SECOND EXERCISE: I EXPERIENCE DECEIT AND SELFISHNESS IN MY LIFE

*I had heard of you by word of mouth,
but now my eye has seen you. . .*

When I spend time on personal sin, I often ask for the grace of self-emptying. I want to see that grace—like an onion skin being peeled. I want to uncover my own sins; I want to come to the true self God has created . . . I quiet myself and relax in the presence of God . . . I acknowledge that I am completely dependent on God.

The Scene:

I see myself standing before God helpless and ashamed.

Grace:

I ask for what I desire: a growing and intense sorrow, even tears, when I recognize how often I participate in the sinful works of society, and grace to realize that through the cross Jesus is setting me free.

Prayer:

i. Psalm 51. "Have mercy on me, O God, in your goodness; in the greatness of your compassion wipe out my offense." I rely on God's goodness and compassion to bring forth wisdom and goodness in my inmost being.

ii. 2 Samuel 11:1-12:13. "Then David said to Nathan, 'I have sinned against the Lord.'" David sinned against God by his adultery with Bathsheba and his murder of her husband.

iii. Romans 7:14-24. "What happens is that I do, not the good I will to do, but the evil I do not intend." I feel shamed by the evil living within my members. . . .

iv. My Personal Sins. I do an inventory of my own personal sins, seeing in them the deceit and hypocrisy that is in them. I may wish to seek reconciliation with someone in particular or with the entire community of Christ's body.

Closing:

Trusting in Mary, the woman of compassion and the mother of Jesus, I ask her to obtain for me the gifts of deep knowledge of my dark and deceitful side, and hatred for sin, insight into how I can be made new, and alertness to let go of anything that stands between me and Jesus. Hand in hand she and I go to Jesus to make the same requests; and with Jesus in turn we go to his Father to ask for these same graces. St. Ignatius calls this the "Triple Colloquy."

Reflections:

The basic struggle of the First Week is between self-gratification and surrender to God. We want a relationship with God, but we want to decide what that relationship will be. Becoming freed from our unhealthy attachments, including our fears and past hurts, is the focus of the First Week. As long as we are controlled by them, we will remain caught between God's spirit of hope and the dark spirit of despair.

This is a time of spiritual conversion. It is hard work. Confronting our blocks and self-attachments is a painful place to be. The basic temptation of the First Week is to give in to discouragement and depression. This is not the work of grace; it is temptation. Nothing has gone wrong. It simply means that the work of the First Week is happening, that the struggle between the spirit of life and the spirit of darkness is taking place in you. Not giving up and remaining faithful to this struggle is the only way to work through it. The best source of strength while doing this is to hang on to the memory of the pure love of God. It is through faithful and utterly honest prayer that we move from the imprisonment of self-attachment into a new inner freedom and life, the goal of the First Week.

Suggestions:

  i. Review your life journey to the present—people, events, places—and look for your patterns of rejecting God's invitations or misusing God's gifts. Become aware of your infidelities to others as well as the addictions in your own life.
 ii. Depression and discouragement are not the goal of this exercise. Becoming more deeply aware of how much God has loved you even in your darkest times will lead to feelings of gratitude and a sense of deliverance from harmful memories and present self-attachments. This is the grace of the First Week.
iii. Prayerfully read *Making Moral Choices During the First Grace (Week)* on pages 124ff.

Have mercy on me, O God, in your goodness;
in the greatness of your compassion wipe out my offense.
Thoroughly wash me from my guilt
and of my sin cleanse me.

—Psalm 51:3-4.

THE THIRD EXERCISE: I EXPERIENCE DECEIT AND SELFISHNESS IN THE WORLD

*I have dealt with great things that I do not understand:
things too wonderful for me, which I cannot know. . . .*

The less I am aware of my own dark side, the more I am a part of society's indifference to and hatred for our sisters and brothers and for our earth's goods. We continue to see our need for God who is always near us with forgiving love . . . I quiet myself and relax in the presence of God . . . I acknowledge that I am completely dependent on God.

The Scene:
I see myself standing in total need of God's loving help.

Grace:
I ask for what I desire: a growing realization and sorrow over the darkness and brokenness in our society.

Prayer:
i. Genesis 3:1-4:16. "The eyes of both were opened, and they realized they were naked." The story of evil is the story of deceit. It is in me and around me . . . .

ii. Isaiah 53:1-12. "He was pierced for our offenses, crushed for our sins." I look on the consequences of sin as I see the Suffering Servant who bears our infirmities . . . .

iii. Hosea 2:4-25. "I will allure her . . . she will say, 'I will go back to my first husband.'" I become aware of God's alluring me back . . . .

iv. Matthew 25:31-46. "Come, you have my Father's blessing . . . out of my sight, you condemned!" I ponder my final blessing . . . .

Closing:

I see Jesus on the cross looking at his people and all creation with compassion and love. What do I wish to say to him?

Reflections:

Ignatius invites us to pray for the grace of "shame and confusion." By this he means a loss of direction, a total loss of face before a situation that cannot be long endured. This grace helps us to see that we cannot save ourselves. Ignatius tried that and once considered suicide. If, however, we keep our eyes on God, then the awareness of our tendencies to selfishness and unfaithfulness opens us to the experience of God's freeing pure love for us.[2]

---

[2] See Carolyn Osiek, R.S.C.J., "The First Week of the Spiritual Exercises and the Conversion of Saint Paul," in David L. Fleming, S.J. (ed.), *Notes on the Spiritual Exercises* (Saint Louis: Review for Religious, 1983), p. 88.

Shame and confusion pass through three stages. The *first stage* is marked by felt guilt over specific acts for which I am responsible. These may be acts of domination and oppression or acts of self-denigration and diminishment. My guilt reflects my responsibility for what I did. The *second stage* is the uncovering of my underlying basic tendency to give in to my dark side, for which I am only partly responsible on the conscious level. A new feeling enters in: helplessness, an inability to do what I want to do in life. The *third stage* reaches the depth at which personal responsibility is no longer at stake. It is the experience of total powerlessness and inability to save one's self. Here it is no longer a question of guilt but of clinging to some memory of God's pure love for me.[3] Ignatius's "shame and confusion" are about not being able to go on living without the hope of being saved by God's freeing love.

Suggestions:

    i. Reflect on the ways the dark spirit moves you. Keep your eyes fixed on God.

    ii. Prayerfully read *Making Moral Choices During the First Grace (Week)* on pages 124ff.

---

[3] Osiek, *loc. cit.,* p. 87.

THE FOURTH EXERCISE: GOD LOVES ME AND DRAWS ME OUT OF DARKNESS AND ALIENATION

*The loving gaze of God watches over the universe,
attentive to the needs of all, active in us and through us. . .*

There is a mystical interconnectedness in all the universe; there is a oneness of all people. People need one another to be whole, to create the whole. We don't lose our identity or originality when in communion with one another; we discover it. We need to find our own creativity; we need interaction to find the place where God wishes each person to be . . . I find myself in the presence of God united to all creation . . . I acknowledge that I am completely dependent on God.

The Scene:

I stand helpless and hopeful before God who loves me just as I am.

Grace:

I ask for what I desire: to live and act in creation and in my particular world as the Spirit makes possible.

Prayer:

i. Baruch 1:13-22. "Pray . . . for we have sinned against the Lord our God." I pray this as a confession of sin by the people, for and with the people of God speaking to God. I pray in the name of my country and in the name of the world. . . .

ii. Isaiah 42:1-9. "Here is my servant whom I uphold." Entering into the consequences of evil, I hear God's all-holy promise. . . .

iii. Ezekiel 37:1-13. "Thus says the Lord God to these bones, 'See! I will bring spirit into you, that you may come to life.'" I see signs of God's spirit of life and hope all around me in the world.

iv. Judith 9:7-14. "You are the God of the lowly, the helper of the oppressed, the supporter of the weak, the protector of the forsaken, the savior of those without hope." This I pray in difficult times for. . . .

Closing:

I find a way to express my thoughts and feelings to God without using words. . . .

Reflections:

It is when we feel helpless before the grip of self-addiction that we are opened to the possibility of new life. It is similar in Alcoholics Anonymous: one must first "hit bottom" before being able to reach out for help. This is a painful place to be, but it is where we learn with the help of God's loving grace that we are not alone, that in acknowledging our helplessness, we discover God's strength and, in God, our own.

In our weakness God's forgiving love is revealed. It is in our worst times that Paul's comment strikes home:

"The Lord said to me, 'My grace is enough for you, for in weakness power reaches perfection.' And so I willingly boast of my weaknesses instead, that the power of Christ may rest on me [2 Cor. 12:9]."

The emphasis throughout this first week is not on how weak and helpless we are, but on how much God loves us. That is why we look at our dark side in full view of God's unconditional love. This is the good news of the Gospel, that God loves us just as we are.

Suggestions:

i. Ask yourself if your experience of sin brings you to hopelessness or to faith.

ii. Pray for God to show you the parts of yourself that you don't want to look at, that you don't love, that God loves.

iii. Prayerfully read *Making Moral Choices During the First Grace (Week)* on pages 124ff.

THE FIFTH EXERCISE: GOD LOVES ME AND
DRAWS ME OUT OF DARKNESS AND ALIENATION

*Therefore I discover what I have said
and repent in dust and ashes. . . .*

I understand better the history of evil in the world and in myself. Satan's tactics led me to forget about God and hide in our contemporary culture. There was no one to denounce this—not even myself. So it was that I myself became partner to evil. I was heavy at heart, but as I contemplated such great evil, a light rose in my heart. Salvation was already at hand . . . I quiet myself and relax in the presence of God . . . I acknowledge that I am completely dependent on God.

The Scene:
I see myself helpless and waiting, standing before a loving God.

Grace:
I ask for what I desire: intense sorrow for my self-deceptions and self-centeredness as I gaze upon the loving, forgiving face of God.

Prayer:
> i. Ezekiel 34:11-17. "The lost I will seek out, the strayed I will bring back, the injured I will bind up, the sick I will heal." I hear the promise of God that I am not lost, that I will be saved even in my weakness and brokenness. . . .

> ii. Ezekiel 36:24-31. "I will give you a new heart and place a new spirit within you . . . you shall be my people, and I will be your God." Entering into the consequences of evil, I hear the all-holy God's promise, "I shall re-establish you on your own soil."

> iii. Luke 7:36-50. "Her many sins are forgiven her because of her great love." I see Jesus continually reaching out to the sinner, to those seeking forgiveness. What he asks from us are not sacrifices but love. . . .

> iv. Luke 15:11-32. "Let us eat and celebrate because this son of mine was dead and has come back to life. He was lost and now is found." God knows us and will do all things to help us realize our dignity.

Closing:
> Aware of the mercy of God and the saving action of God in my own life and world, I turn to God in gratitude and praise. . . .

Reflections:

It is the work of sin to blind us, to keep us from going into our dark side. This causes us to waste energy and time by avoiding those parts of ourselves where we feel anger and hurt and fear. Any turning in on self raises doubts in us and holds us back from the fuller participation in life that we all desire.

The grace of the First Week is the experience of delivery from the paralysis of alienation and despair. It is the life-changing discovery of a God who loves us just as we are. This is the power that frees us from the darkness in our lives, and the healing that comes is not just of our past despair but of our present alienation and spiritual desolation. This is the grace of the First Week. What spontaneously arises in our hearts is gratitude.

Suggestions:

i. Express in your journal or in some other way the grace of healing and love you received during this First Grace (Week).

ii. Celebrate reconciliation in your community with a ritual.

iii. Prayerfully read *Making Moral Choices During the First Grace (Week)* on pages 124ff.

SUMMARIZING THE
FIRST WEEK EXPERIENCE

Gratitude for Being Loved Just As I Am

What is the First Week about? It is about experiencing God's unconditional love which makes real the call of the First Principle and Foundation to orient our whole lives to choose what better leads us to the deepening of God's life in us.

If the First Week is about God's love, why do we look at sin? Because it is there. Whether we look at it or not, the reality of evil is all around us. The work of the First Week is to help us recognize and be freed from this dark side of life by drawing us more deeply into the reality of God's love. The more deeply we move into what is of love, the more we move away from what is not, which is sin. It is only in the light of God's love that we are able to see the shadows of non-love: selfishness, despair, and disrespect.

Is the focus here to remain primarily on the dark side of life? No, we look at our past blocks and deceits only until we discover our present alienations. That is the work of the First Week, to recognize where we are not yet loving toward ourselves and others. There is no value in wallowing in our dark past. Simply dwelling on that is narcissistic and destructive. What we seek is to be saved from our present alienations and destructive patterns.

What is the grace-gift of the First Week? The gift is the deliverance from our past dead weights and numbness and becoming more fully alive. It is the move from anger and blame to equanimity and peace. Whether this is a strong emotional experience or simply the desire for it, the grace is being given. This is a gift of God and is given only in God's good time.

INTEGRATION OF THE
FIRST GRACE (WEEK)

Gratitude for Being Loved Just As I Am

The question at the end of the First Week is, "Have I accepted the truth that even though I sometimes act out of deceit and lack of love, and that on my own I cannot rid myself of this dark side of my life, I am still unconditionally forgiven and loved by God just as I am?" Saying "no" to this question indicates that I need to continue praying for this grace; I am still turned in on myself, trapped by the alienation of sin. Saying "yes" to it, even though I have not yet fully experienced it, indicates the grace has been given. It is evidenced by a largeness of spirit. This is the grace of the First Week. The experience is one of gratitude.

We never completely "have" this grace; we are always growing into it. So the grace of the First Week continues to grow throughout the Second, Third, and Fourth Weeks of the Exercises, as well as during the rest of our lives.

> *Jesus, I feel within me*
> *a great desire to please you;*
> *but, at the same time,*
> *I feel totally incapable of doing this*
> *without your special light and help,*
> *which I can expect only from you.*
> *Accomplish your will within me—*
> *even in spite of me.*[4]

---

[4] St. Claude La Colombiere, S.J.; see Harter, *op. cit.,* p. 22.

PART THREE

THE SECOND GRACE (WEEK): COMPANIONSHIP WITH JESUS

THE REIGN OF GOD

Once, on being asked . . .
when the Reign of God would come,
He replied,
"You cannot tell by careful watching
when the Reign of God will come.
Neither is it a matter of reporting
that it is 'here' or 'there.'
The Reign of God is already
in your midst."

—Luke 17:20-21

TRANSITION INTO THE SECOND
GRACE (WEEK)

Once, on being asked . . . when the Reign of God would come, Jesus replied: "You cannot tell by careful watching when the Reign of God will come. Neither is it a matter of reporting that it is 'here' or 'there.' The Reign of God is already in your midst."

EXERCISE: A MEDITATION ON
"THE REIGN OF GOD"

The ministry of Jesus's words and actions is the Reign of God. He uses parables (images, stories, wise sayings) to describe this reign, to whet our curiosity, and to touch us so that we can experience what the Reign of God is and decide whether we want to be a part of it. I quiet myself and remember that I am in the presence of God . . . I give all my attention to prayer . . . I open my heart to the Source of Life.

The Scene:

Ignatius, using the cultural imagery of his time, develops a parable on the Reign of God. He calls it "The Call of the King." In it he describes two kings (you may substitute prophet, leader, or some other meaningful image). The first is an earthly king inviting his followers to come after him on some great worldly quest for power and glory.

He then describes Jesus as the heavenly king inviting his followers to accompany him in conquering the world for God. The point of this parable is that if the earthly king is worthy to be followed, so much more is Jesus.

Grace:

I ask for what I desire: to hear Jesus's invitation and be ready to respond with my whole self to what He desires.

My Own Personal Parable:

i. From inside myself I sit quietly waiting for an invitation . . . wanting not to miss it . . . wanting to move beyond my perceived limits . . . letting the Spirit open my mind and heart to possibilities . . . letting Jesus reveal . . . .

ii. I play around with possibilities . . . scripture . . . symbol . . . story . . . experiences of the past few weeks . . . a way of finding myself whole and alive.

iii. I go to a place that is sacred for me and sit in the presence of Christ. I hear Him speak, possibly in words like these: "My friend, it is time to stop asking when or where the Reign of God will appear. Read the signs of the times. I am here. I want you to be with me living this Reign. Please see and change whatever you need to change so that you will be free to share with me in this Reign."

iv. What is my parable? I take up my journal, use paints, clay, music, or whatever medium I prefer and begin to portray my own personal parable on the Reign of God in my life—of how I want to be fully with Jesus and let Him shape my life.

Closing:

As I consider my response to this invitation from Jesus, I speak to Him about it. I may want to make an offering in some way.

Reflections:

The beginning of the Second Week looks to Christ to save us. It calls us to follow Him, which entails growing into a personal relationship with Him. His invitation is not only to be with Him, but to be like Him—so that, by sharing in his work and suffering, we will share in the joy of his risen life.

This meditation is about living justice, love, and peace. The overriding call is, "Change your hearts; the Reign of God is at hand!" We do not choose the Reign of God; we are invited into it.

Suggestions:

i. Read Matthew 5:3-13 and also Matthew 13. These are descriptions of the Reign of God.

ii. In the light of all of the above, write out your current personal offering to Jesus.

iii. Now write out the offering you would *like* to make to Jesus.

iv. Let your prayer rise out of the difference between the two.

THE FIRST EXERCISE:
THE INCARNATION

The Word Became Flesh . . . .

I look at people all over the earth: various groups working, playing, fighting, struggling, laughing, being born, dying. I watch God seeing all this, and I wonder what God feels. I open my heart to the Source of All Being who wishes to save the whole world . . . I quiet myself and relax in the presence of God . . . I open my heart to the Source of Life.

The Scene:
I see the village of Nazareth in Galilee and the house where Mary lives. She is in one of the rooms, when suddenly....

Grace:
I ask for what I desire . . . an intimate knowledge of the Word who has become flesh for us, that I may love Him more deeply and follow Him more closely.

Prayer:
i. Luke 1:26-38. "'Blessed are you among women . . . Let it be done to me as you say.'" I hear the angel's announcement and listen carefully for Mary's response. The dialogue begins. . . .

ii. Luke 1:39-45. "When Elizabeth heard Mary's greeting, the baby leapt in her womb. Elizabeth . . . cried out in a loud voice: 'Who am I that the mother of my Lord should come to me?'" As the two mothers meet, I feel with them the burst of joy in the life coming among us.

iii. Luke 1:46-56. "'My being proclaims the greatness of the Lord, my spirit finds joy in God my Savior . . . He has deposed the mighty from their thrones and raised the lowly to high places.'" I stand with Mary and allow my being to proclaim the greatness of God . . . .

iv. Luke 1:56. "Mary remained with Elizabeth about three months and then returned home." I am struck at seeing Mary now spiritually transformed, yet continuing on with very ordinary and immediate concerns . . . .

Closing:

According to the light received, I speak to Jesus's Father, Jesus, the Spirit, or to Mary; and I ask for the grace to follow and live in union with Jesus who became human for me and for the world.

Reflections:

The Second Grace (Week) is about the call to be a follower of Jesus of Nazareth as described in the Beatitudes (Matthew 5:3-13). Now I hear Him calling me into a deep personal relationship with Him, putting off the conventional attitudes of the world and taking on his.

It is possible that you may be experiencing some discouragement in your prayer at this time. You may still be feeling some of the old resentments and negative patterns of behaviors that surfaced during the First Week that you just prayed through. This is a critical time; you may be experiencing a temptation to stop trying to come closer to God. The best way to deal with this is to recognize it for what it is—temptation—and to pray for continued faithfulness to God in your quest. Keep your focus on God, who is loving you just as you are right now, and not on your own weakness and need to be saved. Seen in this way, the experience of your absolute need for God becomes a wonderful grace.

Suggestions:

i. The prayer of the Exercises is now *Contemplation.* It is a work of the heart for love, not of the mind leading to conclusions.

ii. What struck you in this contemplation? How were you most moved? Apply this to your life in the way that seems most fruitful.

iii. Let prayer come to you. Prayer is a work of the heart.

iv. Pray only with those scripture passages that strike you. You need not use them all.

THE SECOND EXERCISE:
BETHLEHEM

. . . and made his dwelling among us . . . .

I recall waiting for someone to be born: the pregnant woman, the adult searching for his "inner-child," the mother-to-be who is single. I let myself be with and be part of the experience. I seek, or I provide a shelter, a place of refuge, a cave . . . I quiet myself and relax in the presence of God . . . I open my heart to the Source of Life.

The Scene:
> I see the inn, the manger, and the shepherds; I feel the atmosphere.

Grace:
> I ask for what I desire: an intimate knowledge of the Word who has become human for us, that I may love Him more deeply and follow Him more closely.

Prayer:
> i. Luke 2:1-7. "'This day in David's city a savior has been born to you, the Messiah and Lord.'" I enter into a place of quiet after a long journey, and become part of what is happening as Jesus is born. . . .

ii. Luke 2:8-20. "[The shepherds] went in haste and found Mary and Joseph, and the baby lying in a manger; once they saw, they understood what had been told them concerning this child." With the shepherds, I am among the first to hear the Good News and respond, "Let us go over to Bethlehem." Once there I understand what had been told concerning this child . . . .

iii. Luke 2:21. "The name Jesus was given the child." With Mary and Joseph I honor Jesus by proclaiming the name He was given by the angel.

iv. Psalm 98. "Sing to the Lord a new song, for he has done wondrous deeds; the Lord has made his salvation known: in the sight of the nations he has revealed his justice." I join in that song . . . .

Closing:

I let the Spirit direct my words as I speak intimately, or quiet my mind and heart to be present with Jesus, or with Mary, or with the Holy One who sent Jesus.

Reflections:

You do not need to experience the grace of each exercise before moving on to the next. The grace of the

First Week continues to grow during the Second Week, and so on. Spiritual growth is not methodical or predictable; what is called for is being present spiritually to what is happening within at the present moment, whether it be attraction or revulsion.

So for instance, I pray even more earnestly—and patiently—to be a companion of Jesus when feeling doubts and resistance to it. For Ignatius, this is to "desire to desire a grace," in this case to desire the desire to be a companion of Jesus. The Exercises assist us in opening ourselves up to the grace that is being sought.

Suggestions:

i. Contemplation is a looking long at Jesus in the Gospels to allow him to enter and transform us here and now.

ii. What struck you in this contemplation? How were you moved? Apply this to your life experiences as seems most fruitful.

iii. Pray repeatedly for the grace to allow Jesus to become the center of your life.

iv. Prayerfully read *Choosing to Follow Christ—Discernment of Spirits During the Second Grace (Week)* on pages 127f.

THE THIRD EXERCISE:
THE TEMPLE AND THE FLIGHT INTO EGYPT

. . . and we have seen his glory . . . .

I recall my childhood, being brought to a "temple," moving to a new place, learning from teachers, from my parents, praying, growing, taking risks, becoming who I am, coming to know Jesus . . . I quiet myself and relax in the presence of God . . . I open my heart to the One who gives me being and life.

The Scene:

The Presentation . . . the Flight into Egypt . . . The Finding in the Temple . . . I see Jesus as infant and boy already summoning me to openness to his call.

Grace:

I ask for what I desire: an intimate knowledge of Jesus who grew through the events of his particular human life, that I may love him more deeply and follow him more closely in the life that is mine.

Prayer:

i. Luke 2:22-40. "'This child is destined to be the rise and fall of many.'" Coming into the temple I see and hear amazing things about the baby. I draw close to Mary as she hears Simeon's words . . . .

ii. Matthew 2:13-23. " 'Get up, take the child and his mother, and flee to Egypt.' " Responding to a dream, faithful Joseph gets up and flees with Mary and the child to Egypt. I think about going with them . . . .

iii. Luke 2:41-52. " 'Did you not know I had to be in my Father's house?' " The anxious parents come upon their missing son in the temple and hear his mysterious self-revelation. I watch them . . . .

iv. Psalm 27. "One thing I ask of the Lord, this I seek: to dwell in the house of the Lord all the days of my life." Show me, O Lord, your way; show me where you dwell . . . .

Closing:

In the presence of mystery, I address Jesus's Abba, or Mary, or Jesus, allowing my heart to spill over as the Spirit leads . . . .

Reflections:

You may at times experience a movement towards something, a desire for something, but you know not what. You know you want something very much, but you do not know what it is. It is not for this or that; it is a longing and is often accompanied by a sense of well-being. It may be what you are experiencing is the desire for relationship, for union with God. It is quite possible that what you are experiencing is being desired into existence by God, of being desirable.[1]

This is not a time to be concerned about self-worth or goodness. It is a time to allow experience to run its course. Take this experience to prayer, to let God communicate to you what in it is the invitation. This is a time of communication, a time of grace.

Suggestions:

   i. Contemplation is being present to the mystery of the event and to its meaning to me here and now.

   ii. What struck you in this contemplation? How were you moved? Apply this to your life as seems most fruitful.

   iii. Remember the value of jotting down your prayer experiences.

   iv. Prayerfully read *Choosing to Follow Christ—Discernment of Spirits During the Second Week*, on pages 127f.

---

[1] William A. Barry, S.J., *Finding God in All Things* (Notre Dame, Indiana: Ave Maria Press, 1991), p. 37.

THE FOURTH EXERCISE:
THE BAPTISM AND THE TEMPTATION

> *. . . the glory of an only Son coming*
> *from the Father filled with enduring love . . . .*

In the silence and desperation of my struggle to become who I truly am, I go with Jesus as he sets out into the desert to live the life and do the work that he came to accomplish . . . I quiet myself and relax in the presence of God . . . I open my heart to the Source of my life.

The Scene:

The Baptism of Jesus . . . the Temptation in the Desert . . . I see Jesus preparing himself to begin his vocation to reveal the love of the One who sent him. He already knows the price, but his eyes remain fixed on . . . .

Grace:

I ask for what I desire: an intimate knowledge of Jesus coming in the power of the Spirit and tempted as we are, that I may love him more and follow him more closely.

Prayer:

   i. Mark 1:1-11. "'You are my beloved son. On you my favor rests.'" John acknowledges that Jesus is more powerful than himself. I can see that Jesus comes out of the Baptism different from when he went in . . . .

   ii. Jeremiah 1:4-10. "The Lord answered me, 'Say not, <I am too young.> To whomever I send you, you shall go; whatever I command you, you shall speak.'" In spite of my objections, I hear from the beginning of my creation as a human being the call of God to . . . .

   iii. Matthew 4:1-11. "'Away with you, Satan! Scripture has it: <You shall do homage to the Lord your God; God alone shall you adore.>'" The tempter approaches. I recognize my tempter as . . . Jesus turns to me, and says . . . .

   iv. Luke 4:16-22. "'The Spirit of the Lord is upon me . . . to bring glad tidings to the poor, to proclaim liberty to captives, recovery of sight to the blind, and release to prisoners. . . .'" Jesus in the midst of his own people invites me to trust that God is alive, present, and working through human history.

Closing:

As the Spirit leads me, I converse intimately with Jesus about whatever is in my heart, or I remain quiet and at peace.

Reflections:

Central to the experience of the Exercises is what Ignatius refers to as "repetition of prayer." It is a practice of returning to pray over those points in a previous prayer in which I experienced something.

This is a pattern established at the beginning of this Second Week. Ignatius tells us that when contemplating a mystery of Christ, "We should pay attention to and dwell upon those points in which we have experienced greater consolation or desolation or greater spiritual appreciation" (#62 in the Exercises). Returning to these particular points in subsequent prayer tends to a growing simplification in prayer and increasing clarity about where the Spirit is leading. Prayer becomes less a matter of ideas and images and more of simple Presence. Where this prayer is leading becomes the fruit of this Presence.

Suggestions:

i. In contemplation, we allow the scene in the Gospel to produce its effect in us here and now.

ii. What struck you in this contemplation? How were you moved? Apply this to your life as seems fruitful.

iii. Remember to pray out of your own real-life experiences. How does this contemplation relate to what is happening in your life?

iv. Prayerfully read *Choosing to Follow Christ—Discernment of Spirits During the Second Week* on pages 127f.

THE FIFTH EXERCISE: A MEDITATION ON TWO WAYS (STANDARDS) OF LIVING

The Way of the World:
I will give you wealth, prestige, privilege,
and power over others. . . .

The Way of Jesus:
Blessed are the poor, the lowly, and the
persecuted because of me. . . .

In the Way of the World, the "haves" are the included, dominant, controlling, closed, superior, respected, and harsh. The "have nots" are the excluded, subservient, manipulated, controlled, inferior, ignored, and injured. The world's way is the way of deceit and manipulation.

In the Way of Jesus, the blessed are poor in spirit, sorrowing, lowly, hungering and thirsting for holiness, showing mercy, single-hearted, peacemakers, persecuted for holiness, and insulted because of him. Jesus's way is the way of mercy and love . . . I quiet myself and relax in the presence of God . . . I open my heart to the Source of Life.

The Scene:
I see two charismatic leaders with opposite approaches:
The *Tempter* entices followers to seek wealth, privilege, power over others, and self-centeredness;
Jesus invites followers to union with him who is poor, opposed to the worldly values of the Tempter, and in loving relationship with the Holy One who sent him.

Grace:

I ask for what I desire: to become free of worldly values which oppose the Reign of God, and to become one with Christ in his work of revealing his Father's love.

Prayer:

i. Matthew 6:19-34. " 'Look at the birds in the sky.' "

The Gospel "rich" are those who embrace the ways of the world by accumulating, not sharing, idolizing wealth, power, and prestige. Is my spontaneous preference towards these rich? Does my lifestyle seek their well-being? In what ways?

The Gospel "poor" are those whose basic needs are not met, who are victims of injustice, especially the rejected, the marginalized, the voiceless. Is my spontaneous preference towards these poor? Does my lifestyle seek their well-being? In what ways?

ii. Matthew 19:16-39. "The [rich] young person went away sad."

I find myself in my world. I enter into my own experience of having the ability to meet my needs.... I focus on basic material, psychological, and social needs.

What is my experience of *not* having my needs met... being a victim of injustice . . . being dismissed and discounted . . . being marginalized and voiceless?

What is my experience of "having" what I need and possibly more . . . having my rights respected . . . being in a nurturing relationship . . . speaking and being heard?

iii. Matthew 5:1-12. "The Beatitudes."

I find Jesus in my world and I look at him, the Happy One. I wait for his word. He speaks first in who he is, and then in what he does and says. I read the Beatitudes and enter into Jesus's experience of happiness. I am among his disciples as he begins to teach us how to become happy. Seeing the Reign alive in Jesus, I trust in his way of happiness . . . . I want to be like Jesus . . . I want to work with him in making God's Reign actual today in the ordinary routine of everyday life.

Closing:

When something challenging is being considered, Ignatius often suggests praying a "triple colloquy" (conversation) with Mary, Jesus, and Jesus's Father. I may wish to pray as follows:

I speak to Mary, and I ask her to pray with me and for me. I talk about the Reign of God, and about how I see Jesus bringing about the Reign. I ask her to obtain for me the blessing of following Jesus radically as she did in the way of the Beatitudes. I end with the *Hail, Mary.*

Mary and I speak with Jesus and ask him to obtain this same grace for me from Abba ("Father," or whatever name I prefer). I end with the *Soul of Christ.*

Jesus, Mary, and I speak to Abba and ask for this same grace. I end with the *Lord's Prayer.*[2]

---

[2] Adapted from Sisters of Providence, *The Love of Christ Impels Us: Providence Retreat in Everyday Life* (Spokane, WA, 1991), p. 92.

Reflections:

The paradoxical condition for following Jesus is that in losing our life for his sake, we find it. It is as Paul says, that we must empty ourselves to be filled with Christ. Not having things his way is what Peter had to learn before he could enter into Jesus's way.

This meditation makes explicit the value system of Jesus. His way is the way of poverty, humiliation, and suffering. We do not seek poverty, humiliation, and suffering for themselves; we seek Jesus who is poor, rejected, humble. It is Jesus who saves us. It is in feeling diminished and discounted that I am laid bare to the full embrace of God.

Suggestions:

i. Relate this meditation to today's reality. See which value systems the daily news presents. See your life and work. Do you represent the Way of the World or the Way of Jesus?

ii. Pray to be invited into the Way of Jesus.

iii. Prayerfully read *Choosing to Follow Christ—Discernment of Spirits During the Second Week* on pages 127f.

THE SIXTH EXERCISE: A MEDITATION ON THREE CLC COMMUNITIES

> *It is not WHAT these communities decide,*
> *but HOW FREE they are to decide.*

I quiet myself and relax in the presence of God . . . I open my heart to the Source of Life.

The Scene:

Three Christian Life Communities are each holding special meetings trying to decide what to do with $10,000 that was given to each of them "for the benefit of CLC." Should they keep it for the benefit of their own community or send it somewhere where it would benefit a larger number of CLC members?

Grace:

I ask for what I desire, namely the interior freedom to choose only what is for the greater glory of God and to trust that what God desires for me reveals my truest, most meaningful self.

Meditation:

i. The *first community* wants to get over its uncomfortableness. They pray individually and together to know what to do. They schedule meetings to talk about what to do with this money. They discuss this regularly, sometimes talking far into the night. This continues for a long period of time. By the time the last community member dies, they have prayed and talked a lot, but they have never done anything with the money.

ii. The *second community* likewise wants to overcome its restless feelings about the money. They pray individually and as a group to know what to do. They put some money into one community project suggested by one member, some goes for some need proposed by another. They take action, but the community keeps control of the money, asking God to bless what they do with it. They never come to the peace of knowing what *God* wants them to do with it.

iii. The *third community* talks about the money. They also pray individually and as a group about what to do with it. However, in all their praying and talking, their one concern is to use the money as God inspires them. Their attitude is, "We will either keep the money or give it to a larger group. The money doesn't really belong to this community, so we'll be God's servants in disposing of it in whatever way God inspires us to act."

Closing:

I pray the Triple Colloquy (see above, page 47):

I speak to Mary, and I ask her to pray with me and for me that I might be close to Jesus: first in spiritual poverty and even in actual poverty, if God would choose me for this, and second in union with him and with all who are not treated with human dignity. I end with the *Hail, Mary.*

Mary and I speak with Jesus and ask him to obtain for me
from his Father these same graces. I end with the *Soul
of Christ.*

Jesus, Mary, and I speak to God, whom Jesus calls
"Abba," and ask for these same graces. I end with the
Lord's Prayer.[3]

Reflections:

The earlier meditations on "The Reign of God" at the
beginning of the Second Grace (Week) and on "The Two
Ways (Standards) of Jesus and the Tempter" specify the
nature of God's Realm. The thrust of this meditation is to
look now at us and our inner dispositions, and to discover
and react against hidden resistances to the call of Jesus's
Father. Our prayer is to make our interior, affective
detachment so real that we can make choices in our daily
lives free of compulsions and attachments, for God's
service alone. This is an effort to experience our total and
absolute dependence on God alone.

Suggestions:

i. Pray to see with which of the three CLC communities you
identify.

ii. Relate this to the realities of your daily life: your job,
family, possessions. Where are your freedoms? Where
are your disordered attachments?

iii. Continue the daily Examen of Consciousness, reflecting
prayerfully over your day, seeing the values and spirits
moving you.

---

[3] Adapted from *The Love of Christ Impels Us,* p. 101.

THE SEVENTH EXERCISE:
TEACHINGS

We are gathered by God. . . .

My own experience of friendship, mutually sharing in special, deep, and personal ways, may be where I discover what it is or could be for me to follow Jesus . . . I quiet myself and relax in the presence of God . . . I open my heart to the Source of my life.

The Scene:

I see Jesus moving about among the people, opening himself to them, and I see how they in turn open themselves to him.

Grace:

I ask for what I desire: an intimate knowledge of Jesus, that I may love him more deeply and follow him more closely.

Prayer:

i. John 1:35-49. "'Rabbi . . . where do you stay?' 'Come and see.'" Two of John's disciples are directed to the "Lamb of God," and they accept his invitation to spend time with him. I follow along. . . .

ii. John 2:1-12. "Cana . . . 'Do whatever he tells you' . . . They did as he instructed them." Mary was the first to respond in faith to the personal love of Jesus and to share in his compassion. She is our model of discipleship, our help, our sure guide. . . .

iii. John 4:4-30. "The woman left her jar and went off into the town . . . 'Come and see.'" Jesus calls the woman to worship in spirit and in truth. She is immediately compelled to go into the town and tell this to others, an early apostle of Jesus. And I?

iv. Luke 10:38-42. "Mary seated herself at the Lord's feet and listened to his words." Jesus challenges Martha to let go of her anxiety and to experience the oneness of being and doing. He then turns and challenges me....

Closing:

As one who is invited into an intimate companionship, I share with Jesus, with Mary, and with the other disciples who come to me.

Reflections:

It is possible that doubts and even anxiety can arise about "how real" all this is in one's life out in the "real" world. This is quite natural and is in fact a very good concern. It indicates a growing awareness of the implications of what is going on here. The Spiritual Exercises don't go halfway any more than Jesus went halfway. They are seemingly relentless in their pursuit of total trust in and abandonment into God.

This process of "letting go" takes time. It is the hardest thing to do, but it should be our main effort: to place our well-being into the hands of another. What is happening is that we are becoming rooted in faith. The secret to letting this happen is fidelity—faithfulness to prayer. This occurs through the slow, gradual, peaceful rhythm of the Exercises. It leads us to a purification in our manner of praying and interior listening, helping us in our quest to remain calm in the hands of God and to face openly what kills life in us.

Suggestions:

i. Contemplation of scripture does not bring Jesus into my life; it brings me into his.

ii. Take time to exchange at least once a week reflections on your prayer with your spouse or a trusted friend.

iii. Prayerfully read *Choosing to Follow Christ—Discernment of Spirits During the Second Week* on pages 127f.

THE EIGHTH EXERCISE:
HEALINGS

. . . your faith has saved you . . . .

Where Jesus is in the midst of people, there is a meeting of humanity and God. There is life. I see this now in my neighborhood, at work, on the road, in church, at the shopping center—humanity and God . . . I quiet myself and relax in the presence of God . . . I open my heart to the source of my life.

The Scene:
I see Jesus walking the dusty roads, meeting people, tireless in reaching out to them, responding to their needs out of love.

Grace:
I ask for what I desire: an intimate knowledge of the humanity of Christ so that I may love him more deeply and follow him more closely.

Prayer:
i. Luke 8:43-48. "'Daughter, it is your faith that has cured you. Now go in peace.'" The woman in the crowd touches Jesus and her hemorrhage stops. She asserts herself publicly with complete trust in Jesus. This says to me. . . .

ii. Luke 9:10-17. "'Why do you not give them something to eat yourselves?'" Jesus looks around at the hungry today . . . so many. "Why do you not give them something to eat yourself?"

iii. Mark 10:46-52. "'Be on your way. Your faith has healed you.'" Jesus asks me, "What do you want me to do for you?"

iv. Luke 19:1-10. "'Zacchaeus, hurry down. I mean to stay at your house today.'" Zacchaeus goes out of his way to see Jesus, who in response comes to him in his own home for dinner. Jesus comes to me in . . . .

Closing:
Familiar friends can talk for a long time about the simplest things, or they can just be together. I am going to spend some time with Jesus. I want to tell him . . . .

Reflections:
Jesus had an amazing capacity to bond with people much more swiftly and deeply than the ordinary dynamics of human relationships make possible. He could change strangers completely and quickly. He looked past initial impressions and saw into their hearts. He looked at people, felt their presence, empathized with their plight with a love that brought deep insight and bonding. He viewed people with a love that revealed their hearts to

him, and he shared his own heart in return.[4]

It can happen that you begin sensing Jesus's wanting to be your companion more than you want to be his. This can be a surprising thought. Jesus wants friends and companions. Just as he reveals himself to us, so too he wants us to reveal ourselves to him. It is odd, even hard, to think of Jesus as actually wanting our friendship, a friendship that is mutual. "I no longer call you servants... Instead I have called you friends, for everything that I learned from my Father I have made known to you (Jn. 15:15)."

Suggestions:

i. What struck you in this contemplation? How were you moved? Apply this to your life as seems fruitful.

ii. Remember to keep praying for the grace to know Jesus, to love him, and to follow him more closely. If you do not desire this, pray to desire it.

iii. Prayerfully read *Choosing to Follow Christ—Discernment of Spirits During the Second Week* on pages 127f.

---

[4] William R. Callahan, *Noisy Contemplation* (Hyattsville, MD: Quixote Center, 1994).

THE NINTH EXERCISE:
TEACHINGS

. . . where the needs call us . . . .

Being needed sometimes calls forth from me the ability to do more than I would have thought possible, and I feel amazed and grateful to be able to help. At other times I struggle with whether I can or want to help, so I turn to Jesus . . . I quiet myself and relax in the presence of God . . . I open my heart to the Source of my life and the lives of people in need.

The Scene:
>   I see Jesus stopping and talking with people who ask him questions and listen carefully to his answers. He is simple and direct.

Grace:
>   I ask for what I desire: an intimate knowledge of Jesus, that I may love him more and follow him more nearly.

Prayer:
>   i. Luke 10:25-37. "'And who is my neighbor?'" When an attorney asks Jesus what to do to attain eternal life, he hears about his neighbor.

ii. Mark 7:24-30. "'Let the children of the household satisfy themselves at table first.'" The Greek woman begs Jesus to expel the demon from her daughter, and he appears to put her off. When I beg Jesus to expel my demons, he sometimes . . . .

iii. Luke 10:1-11. "'I am sending you as lambs in the midst of wolves.'" Jesus's instructions to the seventy-two are simple and direct. Where is he sending me . . . .

iv. Luke 8:1-3. "He journeyed through towns and villages, preaching and proclaiming the good news of the Reign of God." Committed women and men follow Jesus not only in seeking the well-being of others but also in honoring themselves.

Closing:
I speak with Jesus about how he listened to the Spirit in the calls of people around him, and I let him teach me his way of responding.

Reflections:
"We who ask to know Jesus in order to love him more and follow him more closely experience a very complex man. He seems to know God intimately and so can act with compassion and healing even in defiance of customs and religious laws. He is not afraid of controversy. He draws great crowds not only because of his miracles, but

also because of his message. He seems to bring out the fierce animosity and fear of the demons. Getting close to this man may be a dangerous thing. People who ask to know him better will experience both attractions and repulsions as they begin to realize the possible consequences of intimacy."[5]

Life in Jesus is strong and gentle, loving others and loving ourselves. Seeking others' and our own self-worth and freedom can bring out animosity and fear. It is in friendship with Jesus that I too can act courageously and with forgiveness.

Suggestions:

   i. Contemplation is about falling more deeply in love with Jesus.

   ii. What struck you in this contemplation? How were you moved? Apply this to your life as seems fruitful.

   iii. What are your attractions and repulsions regarding this man? Where are they coming from? Name them. Pray over them.

   iv. Prayerfully read *Choosing to Follow Christ—Discernment of Spirits During the Second Week* on pages 127f.

---

[5] Barry, *op. cit.,* p. 94.

THE TENTH EXERCISE: A MEDITATION ON THREE RESPONSES OF LOVE

The Love of Fidelity, Concern, and Identification with Jesus

This meditation builds on the meditations on "The Reign of Christ" (page 30) and on "The Two Standards of Living of the World and of Jesus" (page 45). The point of this meditation is to continue to deepen in our hearts the total offering of ourselves we have made to Christ . . . I quiet myself and relax in the presence of God . . . I open my heart to the Source of my life, acknowledging my dependence on God for all that I have and am.

Grace:

I ask for what I desire: a deeper and more generous response to God in love.

Prayer:

i. First Response: The Love of Fidelity.

This is the way of simple faithfulness. I will never do anything seriously wrong to exclude God from my life. This level is expressed in common and ordinary ways, such as raising one's family in a Christian way, not seeking personal gain at another's expense, or in not totally discounting self to please others. This is the way of the commandments. This level shows obedience to God. Who models this level for me? Who models this in the Gospel? Is this the level God is calling me to?

ii. Second Response: The Love of Concern.

This is the way of personal detachment and love, of total surrender, of an unwillingness to offend God in even the slightest way. The desire in all choices is the love of God. The basic concern is the service and praise of God in others and in myself. This is the way of those, whether religious or lay, who discover personal fulfillment in the care of others. These are the ones who seek to live in conscious union with God. This is the way of active openness (what Ignatius refers to as "indifference of the will") to God.

This level shows deep and generous love of God. Who models this level for me? Who models this in the Gospel? Is this the level God is calling me to?

iii. Third Response: The Love of Identification with Jesus.

This is the work of the heart, the language of love. This level of union with him is so deep that it leads one to choose poverty in order to be with Christ poor rather than rich, to be considered worthless and a fool for Christ rather than be esteemed as wise and prudent in this world. It is not only about being with Christ, it is being like him. This is a profound level of response, of passionate personal love. This is the way of imitating Christ.

This is a grace of great holiness. Who is it that models this level for me? Who models this in the Gospel? Is this the level God is calling me to?

Closing:

I seek to be more generous in my response to God by praying a "triple colloquy" (see above, page 47):

> I speak to Mary, and I ask her to pray with me and for me that I might be close to Jesus. I pray that if it is God's invitation to me, that I even desire actual poverty to be with Christ poor and to bear insults and contempt out of love for Christ as I reverence and value others for him. I end with a *Hail, Mary.*

> Mary and I speak with Jesus, and ask him to obtain for me from his Father these same graces. I end with a *Soul of Christ* (see page 82).

> Jesus, Mary, and I speak to God, whom Jesus calls Abba, and ask for these same graces. I end with the *Lord's Prayer.*

Reflections:

When making a decision ("election" is Ignatius's term) in the Spiritual Exercises about your life, it is good to repeat the colloquy from the meditation on the "Two Ways of Living" (see page 45). With the gift of grace, it sums up the experiences of the contemplations you have gone through since it was made. This meditation on "Three Responses of Love" establishes the climate of interior freedom to make a decision that, before God, you feel called to make. It seeks to deepen the personal enrichment that comes through total surrender to Jesus.

Suggestions:

 i. Which response of love guides your response to God? What are your blocks to this love? What do you fear you would lose if you were given this grace?

 ii. Recall that if you do not actually feel a desire for the grace of this meditation, you pray to desire it.

 iii. Let your Examination of Consciousness help you see what is happening to you in your prayer. (See below, page 122.)

 iv. Prayerfully read *Choosing to Follow Christ—Discernment of Spirits During the Second Week* on pages 127f.

* * * * * * * * * *

So act, good Jesus,
that in my relationships with whatever neighbor
and in all I do for the furthering of your Father's glory
and the salvation of others,
I form myself in your pattern;
that I be a genuine reflection of your moderation,
gentleness, humility, patience, graciousness, tireless zeal,
in a word, of all your virtues;
and, in order to engrave them in my soul,
live eternally in me.[6]

---

[6] Jean-Pierre Medaille, S.J., in Harter, *Hearts on Fire*, p. 53.

THE ELEVENTH EXERCISE:
HEALINGS AND TEACHINGS

. . . through compassionate liberating action . . . .

Whatever obstacles might be in the way of my accomplishing God's will can be removed by God. I believe this, and sometimes when I enter into prayer and savor the words of Scripture, I can see these obstacles as opportunities for growth . . . I quiet myself and relax in the presence of God . . . I open my heart to the Source of my life.

The Scene:

I watch Jesus healing, challenging, inviting, playing. . . . He is an amazing man, how he deals with such different situations.

Grace:

I ask for what I desire: an intimate knowledge of Jesus, to love him more dearly and to follow him more wholeheartedly.

Prayer:

i. Luke 13:10-17. "'Woman, you are freed from your infirmity.'" A woman who can't stand erect hears Jesus call her. She stands — free. The head of the synagogue objects to her being cured on the sabbath. Jesus sees through him and silences him. I can more easily see the evil of bias, including gender bias. . . .

ii. John 2:13-25. "'Stop turning my Father's house into a marketplace!'" Jesus is consumed with zeal for Abba's house. Get them out of here if they don't respect Abba's house. I ponder this house today . . . .

iii. Luke 18:15-17. "'Let the little children come to me . . . the Reign of God belongs to such as these.'" The disciples did not think that the people should be bringing their children, bothering Jesus. Whom else could Jesus welcome . . . With children we see his heart....

iv. Mark 10:17-25. "'Teacher, what must I do to share in everlasting life?'" The man could not sell what he had and give it to the poor. He went away sad. With God all things are possible. . . .

Closing:

I let the presence of the Holy Spirit within me be a source of compassion and an energy toward accomplishing what I feel called to do, knowing this is the Spirit which animates Jesus. I feel . . . .

Reflections:

Jesus's actions on behalf of others reveal the heart of his love for Abba. It is a simple love that quickly dispels any stress on an individualistic and vertical relationship with God. This love was realized in Jesus's love for his people. It was in his loving care of others that he lived out his love for the One who sent him. It is but one love.

This is unambiguously summarized in the following Scripture passages: "As often as you did it for one of my least brothers or sisters, you did it for me [Matthew 24:40]." And, "If anyone says, 'My love is fixed on God,' yet hates his brother or sister, he is a liar. One who has no love for the sister or brother he has seen cannot love the God he has not seen [1 John 4:20]."

The Spiritual Exercises lead to this all-encompassing love for God's people. The grace of the Exercises is an effective love, calling us into the work of transforming the world (which, of course, includes ourselves), leading all out of the slavery of alienation and self-hatred into the light of authentic relationship and hope. This is the revelation of the meditation on "The Reign of God" which is at the beginning of the Second Grace (Week). This is gift; it is a grace to be prayed for.

Suggestions:
   i. Contemplation does not bring the Gospel down to our level; it lifts us up to the level of the Gospel.
  ii. What struck you in this contemplation? How were you moved? Apply this to your life as seems fruitful.
 iii. What are your blocks to wanting to do as Jesus did? Who are the ones in your life you need the grace to love and serve as he did?
  iv. Pray again the closing prayer of this exercise.
   v. Prayerfully read *Choosing to Follow Christ—Discernment of Spirits During the Second Week* on pages 127f.

THE TWELFTH EXERCISE:
JESUS PRAYED

. . . nourished by contemplative prayer . . . .

Conscious that I am called to live and to pray "in Spirit and in truth," I breathe the invocations, "God of mercies and of love, I believe in you, I hope in you, I love you" . . . I quiet myself in the presence of God . . . I open my heart to the Source of my life.

The Scene:

I see Jesus praying by himself at night up on the mountain. I also see him working hard teaching other people about himself and what he is about . . . .

Grace:

I ask for what I desire: an intimate knowledge of Jesus who lives in me through his Spirit, so that I may love and follow him in freedom.

Prayer:

i. Luke 6:12-16. "Then he went out to the mountain to pray, spending the night in communion with God. At day-break he called his disciples. . . ." Jesus prays all night before choosing his disciples and beginning his public ministry. His actions were infused with prayer. This makes me realize . . . .

ii. Luke 11:1-13. "When you pray, say: 'Our Father. . . .' " This is effective prayer. It encompasses all prayer. It is Jesus's prayer. Mine is . . . .

iii. Luke 21:37-38. "He would . . . leave the city to spend the night on the Mount of Olives." Jesus retreats to be with his Abba and to be nourished by him . . . .

iv. Luke 22:41-46. "He . . . went down on his knees and prayed . . . 'Yet not my will but yours be done.' " Jesus rose from prayer ready to do Abba's will, and the apostles who were sleeping were exhausted with grief. What this tells me is . . . .

Closing:

With Mary, I stand before Jesus listening to his call. I say what rises in my heart. I may pray the "triple colloquy," asking for what my heart desires, if that be God's desire for me (see above. p. 47).

Reflections:

Prayer played a central role in Jesus's life. He prayed prayers and the psalms; he prayed alone, with his disciples, and in the temple; he performed the rituals of an adult, male, lay Israelite. He taught prayer and he persevered in it. His prayer was intimate and heartfelt. ("Abba" is like "Daddy.") He liked to pray at night.

Jesus's sense of direction and ministry were closely related to his frequent withdrawal into prayer. His experiences of prayer are frequently mentioned in the Gospel; and are always oriented to his presence and life in the world.

This is in sharp contrast to the superficial ways of the world, embodied perhaps best in Peter at Caesarea Philippi where he confessed his faith in Jesus (cf. Mark 8:27ff). Peter's prayer was made in good will, but was not grounded in a deep, prayerful faith. Any growth in and work of faith must begin in surrender through prayer to the Holy One. This Peter finally experienced in his tearful repentance for denying Jesus.

Suggestions:

i. What struck you in this contemplation? How were you moved? Apply this to your life as seems fruitful.

ii. In what areas of your life is your surrender in prayer to Jesus's Abba missing?

iii. Prayerfully read *Choosing to Follow Christ—Discernment of Spirits During the Second Week* on pages 127f.

THE THIRTEENTH EXERCISE:
MARY

. . . exemplified by Mary . . . .

When I have a difficult time starting prayer with Scripture, I begin with an experience in my life or in the world, as Mary did. When I am dry with Scripture, it fits where I am in my life. At times when I stay with an experience, a thought from scripture comes . . . I quiet myself and relax in the presence of God . . . I open my heart to the Source of my life . . . with Mary, I treasure all these things and reflect on them in my heart.

The Scene:
> I see Mary already as a young woman confronting incredible challenges in her life. I seek her keeping her eyes on her son.

Grace:
> I ask for what I desire: a personal knowledge of the mysterious Jesus, as Mary had, and a passionate love for him so that I may follow him with my whole heart.

Prayer:
> i. Luke 2:19. "Mary treasured all these things and reflected on them in her heart." I look at what I have treasured in my heart. . . .

ii. Luke 2:35. "'. . . and you yourself [Mary] shall be pierced with a sword. . .'" Mary continues to learn what it means to follow her son. What I have learned from Mary is. . . .

iii. Matthew 12:46-50. "'Whoever does the will of my heavenly Father is brother and sister and mother to me.'" Deep relationships with Jesus are on the level of obedience to Abba. . . .

iv. John 19:25. "Near the cross of Jesus there stood his mother . . . 'This is your son. . . .'" Mary is commissioned as mother of the new humanity. Jesus is commissioning me to . . . .

Closing:

I pray the "triple colloquy" (see above, p. 47). I pray to Mary to help me follow Jesus in the way he chooses for me. With her, I ask Jesus to choose me to follow him in the way that would most please and serve his Father. Then, together we approach our Abba with the same request.

Reflections:

Mary teaches us that through faith promise becomes reality. Her faith took root in daily existence, fully inserted into the life of her people and the social, political, and religious context of her country. She neither took refuge in tranquil contemplation nor did she lose contact with her faith through daily activity. Her faith was echoed in the hard work of her daily life. She was a contemplative in action.

Mary is the model of mission, of service to the Church and the world. She remained strong throughout the adversity her son faced during his public ministry. She was outspoken to the people of her day on behalf of the poor in her *Magnificat*. She was faithful to her son's vision in the face of utter failure on the cross. She continued to nurture the disciples in the upper room during the days that followed the Ascension. Mary's faith is filled with wonder, bold in its commitment to her son's mission, and joyful in its gratitude and simplicity. Mary is as central to the Church of the twenty-first century as she was to that of the first generation.

Suggestions:

　i. Who has Mary been to you? Who would you like her to be?

　ii. What struck you in these contemplations? How were you moved? Apply this to your life as seems fruitful.

　iii. Let your Consciousness Examen help you (see below, page 122).

　iv. Prayerfully read *Choosing to Follow Christ—Discernment of Spirits During the Second Week* on pages 127f.

BEGINNING THE TRANSITION
TO PASCHAL MYSTERY

THE FOURTEENTH EXERCISE:
TRANSFIGURATION

> *. . . Indeed, if we are ever caught up*
> *out of ourselves, God is the reason . . . .*

Sometimes I sense the specialness of my relationship with Jesus, the invitation to come to the mountain top. The happiness of my life, the possibility that if, with open eyes, I face what's in front of me, my consciousness might be transformed and the glory of Christ made visible . . . I quiet myself in the presence of God . . . I open my heart to the truth of God.

The Scene:

I see Jesus transfigured before my eyes. He is beautiful. Like Peter and John I want this never to end. I also see him in very ordinary circumstances, yet still inviting us all to the special blessing of his Father's realm.

Grace:

I ask for what I desire: an intimate knowledge of Jesus who reveals his personal being to those close to him, that I may love him more and follow him more closely.

Prayer:

  i. Mark 9:1-10. "He was transfigured before their eyes and his clothes became dazzlingly white." Jesus comes to us and lifts us up to a high place. We are overcome with awe . . . .

  ii. Psalm 84. "How lovely is your dwelling place." I ponder that "the Lord withholds no good thing from those who walk in sincerity."

  iii. John 14:3. "'I am indeed going to prepare a place for you, and then I shall come back to take you with me, that where I am you also may be.'" I long to be there with him . . . .

  iv. Luke 10:21-22. "'I offer you praise, O Father . . . because what you have hidden from the learned and the clever you have revealed to the merest children.'" Rejoicing with the Holy Spirit, I join with Jesus in prayer of praise . . . .

Closing:

  There are so many things to share with Jesus and to offer to our Abba with him that only the Spirit can express this in me . . . .

Reflections:

  There is a joy and a peace in being a companion with Jesus that never becomes boring or routine. It is a joy that comes out of our having shared our deepest selves with him, including our deepest fears, hopes, and desires. It is in these deepest places that Jesus touches us most. If we are with Jesus at our worst, then there will be no place that he has not touched in us. We will have nothing to fear because there is nothing in us left hidden from him. He will have led us through our darkest valleys. We now know that we can trust him without reservation. This is the joy and peace that comes from being a companion with Jesus.

Having spent this time during the Second Week with him allows this to happen. It is the experience of a special relationship with Jesus, of being "at the top of the mountain," of joy in my life. It is as if I were to open my eyes and face toward what is in front of me, and my consciousness would be transformed and the glory of Christ made visible.

Suggestions:

i. Do a Consciousness Examen of your time with Jesus during this Second Week. What have been your hopes? Your joys?

ii. Take time to write these out, in your journal if you have one. Review them periodically; pray over them frequently. There is still more waiting for you to discover.

iii. Share these with a spiritual director or with a trusted friend. Find an occasion to articulate to someone your grace of the Second Week.

CONTINUING THE TRANSITION
TO PASCHAL MYSTERY

THE FIFTEENTH EXERCISE: LAZARUS;
PERFUMING THE BODY; KILL HIM; HOSANNA!

> *. . . And when we are brought back to our senses,*
> *it is for our sakes . . . .*

Throughout my life there have been times when I've become particularly aware of the seriousness of the commitment that Jesus asks of me, and I have needed to believe in who he is and what he can do. I draw on that belief . . . I quiet myself and relax in the presence of God . . . I open my heart to God, offering this special time, offering myself.

The Scene:

"From this time on, many of his disciples broke away and would not remain in his company any longer. Jesus then said to the Twelve, 'Do you want to leave me too?' [John 6:66-67]."

Grace:

I ask for what I desire: an intimate knowledge of Jesus, that I may love him more and follow him with faith and courage.

Prayer:

    i. John 11:1-44. "'Lord, if you had been here, my brother would never have died.'" Jesus was troubled in spirit, moved by the deepest emotions. Jesus grieves over our grief . . . .

    ii. Matthew 26:6-13. "'By pouring this perfume on my body, she has contributed toward my burial preparation.'" The disciples don't understand the woman's preparation for Jesus's death. I ponder this . . . .

    iii. John 11:45-54. "From that day onward there was a plan afoot to kill him." Jesus cannot move about freely among those who reject him . . . .

    iv. Matthew 21:1-17. "The huge crowd . . . kept crying out, 'Hosanna!' Jesus . . . overturned the money changers' tables and the stalls of the dove sellers." With the rest of Jesus's followers, I too wonder, "Who is this?"

Closing:

Perhaps it is with Mary, Mother of Jesus, that I allow my heart to speak most openly and simply to Jesus, praying to follow him even to the end.

Reflections:

Sometimes, after a while the freshness of Jesus's presence wears off, prayer becomes less enthralling, and boredom sets in. Jesus keeps repeating cures and the same message. This doldrum period is best seen as a prelude to another conversion experience. This experience may well be the continuing movement from the gifts of God to God. This may be a continuing revelation of the full implications of what being a follower of Jesus involves.

Often the same conflicts that came up previously around trust in God recur at this point. Real discernment is happening here. Those who reach this point in the Exercises will receive the grace to say "Yes," at any rate to the point of at least desiring the desire to walk with him. There is wisdom in this, because the person now knows that living by Jesus's standards involves the possibility that, like Jesus, (s)he too may suffer. This is being at the gates of Jerusalem on the Sunday of Holy Week.

Suggestions:

i. Pray over the areas of your life where you still do not trust Jesus. Where are the blocks? Where are your attachments?

ii. Do you desire the grace of the Second Week? What don't you desire? Write out your own grace of the Second Week . . . how you want to be a companion with Jesus.

INTEGRATION OF THE
SECOND GRACE (WEEK)

Companionship with Jesus

During this second phase,
you walked with Jesus
through our world
as an intimate friend.

You experienced the mystery
of who Jesus is,
of how Jesus calls you
and chooses you to be,
in your unique way,
the human face of God.

You responded to Christ
as the Spirit led you,
in freedom and love.

You who were chosen
chose Jesus too.
You chose to be with Jesus,
living your particular grace
your beatitude way.[7]

---

[7] Adapted from *The Love of Christ Impels Us*, p. 132.

TRANSITION INTO THE
THIRD GRACE (WEEK)

> *You move into the Passover because*
> *Jesus asks you, his friend,*
> *to walk with him*
> *these last lonely steps*
> *to the cross, and*
> *to labor with him*
> *for the sake of all people*
> *bearing the weight*
> *of the cross.*
>
> *Jesus lets you see him*
> *suffer as humans do,*
> *suffer for love of you,*
> *suffer for love of all*
> *until he dies*
> *in self-giving love*
>
> *Jesus trusts you as friend,*
> *now one of God's family,*
> *to take your stand*
> *at the cross,*
> *to take your stand*
> *with Mary*
> *believing and waiting for*
> *LIFE.*[8]

---

[8] Adapted from *The Love of Christ Impels Us*, p. 143.

SOUL OF CHRIST:

A Contemporary Reading of a Traditional Prayer[9]

Jesus . . . Best Friend
may your soul give life to me,
may your flesh be food for me.
may you warm my hardened heart.

Jesus . . . Best Friend
may your tears now wash me clean,
may your passion keep me strong,
may you listen to my plea.

Jesus . . . Best Friend
may your wounds take in my hurts.
may your gaze be fixed on me,
may I not betray your love.

Jesus . . . Best Friend
may you call me at death's door,
may you hold me close to you,
may you place me with God's saints,
may I ever sing your praise.
Amen.

---

[9] The "contemporary reading" is taken from Fleming, *Draw Me Into Your Friendship*, p. 3.

PART FOUR

THE THIRD GRACE (THIRD WEEK): SHARING IN JESUS'S PASSION

> *. . . and the high priests and scribes*
> *began to look for some way to dispose of him. . . .*

John says, "'I give you a new commandment.'" New? He doesn't just say to love; rather, he says, "Love one another; be a new community; be in communion with all the other disciples." Luke says, "'Now share this cup among you.'" It is about community. Jesus is community-conscious . . . I quiet myself and relax in the presence of God . . . I open my heart to the Source of my life, even in suffering.

The Scene:
   I can see Jesus with his companions sharing the Passover meal. I can tell that everyone knows there is something different about this meal.

Grace:
   I ask for what I desire: deep love and compassion for Jesus, so that I want to go to Calvary with my friend, even as I know he is suffering for me.

Prayer:

    i. Luke 22:14-24. "'This is my body to be given for you... this cup is the new covenant in my blood, which will be shed for you.'" Jesus longs to share this passover with his friends. I am his friend . . . .

    ii. John 13:21-30. "'I tell you solemnly, one of you will betray me . . . ;' he dipped the morsel, then . . . gave it to Judas . . . 'Be quick about what you are to do.'" Satan entered into Judas's heart. I am there . . . .

    iii. Mark 14:27-31. "' . . . this very night, before the cock crows twice, you will deny me three times.'" Satan entered into Peter's heart. I am there . . . .

    iv. John 13:1-11. "He poured water into a basin and began to wash his disciples' feet and dry them . . . ." Then he comes to me . . . .

Closing:

From the depths of my feeling, or from my emptiness, I speak to and listen to my loving friend.

Reflections:

This is the beginning of the Third Week of the Exercises. It is about communion; the language is now that of lover. The grace of the First Week is the experience of being loved and forgiven by God—just as I am. That of the Second Week is learning about Jesus, of growing intimacy with him, leading to the desire not only to follow him but to be like him. The grace of the Third Week is communion with him. I am his beloved. I become one with him, entering even into his sufferings as one present to a dying friend. My response to the grace of communion is "Yes."

In considering my sinfulness during the First Week, the focus was on what my infidelity cost Jesus. The motivation for my love for him came out of an exterior motivation—how I am saved by what he did for me. In the Third Week, the focus is now within me: how I wish to share in Jesus's Passion out of love for him. This is an interior motivation.

Suggestions:

i. Stay in the spirit of Jesus's Passion by frequently recalling the Scriptural readings given above.

ii. If you feel dry and indifferent during prayer, you are actually experiencing the grace of Jesus's Passion. He too felt this. Sharing in Jesus's sorrow is a grace to be prayed for. Stay with him. Embrace whatever you feel and keep your eyes on him. Let the mind rest and the heart speak.

iii. What do you desire? What do you not desire?

THE SECOND EXERCISE:
JESUS'S AGONY

> *. . . Like a lamb led to slaughter . . .*
> *he was silent and opened not his mouth . . . .*

At times I have thought of the Passion of Jesus as past history, but now I see or read about the unjust and cruel treatment of Jesus every day. There is so much violence and terror around us. It is often difficult to accept the dying Jesus when I see so much misery and suffering. The sin of injustice hurts a lot, and it is around us. . . I quiet myself and become aware of how much I am in the presence of God . . . Reverently I offer this time of prayer.

The Scene:
   I stay with the disciples, watching from a distance Jesus filled with fear and distress.

Grace:
   I ask for what I desire: deep compassion and love for Jesus who allows himself out of love for me to be treated so.

Prayer:

    i. Luke 22:39-46. "'Pray that you may not be put to the test' . . . In his anguish . . . his sweat became like drops of blood . . . 'Pray that you may not be subjected to the trial.'" Even in his agony, he shows concern for his followers. I reflect on my own concern . . . .

    ii. Mark 14:43-52. "'Rabbi!' . . . At this they laid hands on him and arrested him." All deserted him and fled. I....

    iii. Matthew 26:57-68. "Many false witnesses took the stand." With Peter I sit down to watch the outcome. We have little to say to each other . . . .

    iv. Mark 14:66-72. "[Peter] began to curse, and to swear, 'I do not even know the man you are talking about!'. . . he broke down and began to cry." Peter suddenly leaves, and I feel . . . .

Closing:

    Seeing Jesus like this, I may want to do something for him. I bring my choices into conversations with him, if that seems right. I let my heart speak.

Reflections:

The Passion of Jesus has two faces. One is that of the Suffering Servant:

There was in him no stately bearing to make us look at him, nor appearance that would attract us to him . . . He was spurned and avoided by men . . . he was pierced for our offenses, crushed for our sins . . . like a lamb to the slaughter . . . oppressed and condemned he was taken away . . . he was cut off from the land of the living . . . he surrendered himself to death and was counted among the wicked . . . [Isaiah 53:1-12].

"My God, my God, why have you forsaken me? All who see me scoff at me; they mock me with parted lips, they wag their heads . . . indeed, many dogs surround me; a pack of evildoers closes in upon me. They have pierced my hands and my feet; I can count all my bones . . . they divide my garments among them, and for my vesture they cast lots [Psalm 22]."

Jesus's Passion appears to be a series of cruel events; his most intimate friends deserted him, and his life appeared as utter failure. This is a frightening darkness to experience. The prayer during the Third Week is to share in the feelings of Jesus during his Passion. Previous closeness to him may now be gone, and the proven methods of touching him fail. The temptation is again to desert him, even in his Passion. This "darkness over the whole land" just comes; our task is to remain in communion with him in love.

It is not the work of grace to escape empty feelings. The work of grace is to keep one's eyes fixed on Jesus during this time and remain one with him. This is not a time for analysis or evaluation; it is rather a time for experiencing, for fidelity, for union with him as with a dying friend. Entering into this reality is entering into life at its fullest and experiencing Jesus with deepest empathy and faith.

Suggestions:

i. Stay in the spirit of Jesus's Passion by frequently recalling the Scriptures given above.

ii. Remember that it was Jesus's love, not his suffering, that has redeemed us.

iii. Ignatius suggests that one pray in an environment in harmony with the prayer. Here, it may be praying in a darkened room, perhaps rising for prayer during the night, avoiding pleasant thoughts and times, performing penances, listening to Bach's *St. Matthew's Passion*, and so forth. This is not an exercise in masochism. It is driving home the dark power of evil and the unconditional love of Jesus in overcoming it.

The Third Exercise:
The Trial

. . . The love of Christ impels us . . . .

In moments of shared pain and rage and grief, there seems to arise an enormous sob as if the entire universe itself were crying out, "This is not what I intended!" Perhaps it is God's own grief for the pain of the world. And yet at the same time, there is something of great dignity and power that I see in Jesus. He is not helpless; he offers himself to this out of love . . . I quiet myself and become aware that I am in the presence of God . . . with reverent love, I offer God this time of prayer.

The Scene:

I see Jesus standing quietly before his accusers, waiting.

Grace:

I ask for what I desire: deep love and compassion for Jesus, so that I want to go to Calvary with my suffering friend.

Prayer:

i. Matthew 27:3-10. "Then Judas . . . began to regret his action deeply." He is at the point of reconciliation with Jesus, but he . . . .

ii. John 18:28-40. "'Truth! What does that mean?'" After this remark I go out to the crowd . . . .

iii. Mark 15:6-15. "So . . . Pilate released Barabbas to them." He wished to please the crowd. I . . . .

iv. Matthew 27:26-31. "Jesus, however, he first had scourged . . . weaving a crown of thorns they fixed it on his head." I want to reach out to him . . . .

Closing:

In the midst of violence and with effort, Jesus continues to be there for us. I may want to express my desire to be there for him.

Reflections:

The other face to Jesus's Passion, besides being the Suffering Servant, is his love for his Father, without whom his Passion is but a series of cruel events. Jesus's whole life was one of revealing Yahweh. In the Passion he most completely emptied himself to reveal the One who sent him. Calvary was the culmination of his entire life.

Calvary was Jesus's greatest experience. He chose God in his suffering. He trusted Abba as he always did. In his suffering, Jesus revealed Yahweh, who chooses life for his Son on Calvary, as He always does for us. Jesus looked past his sufferings to the Holy One, and Calvary made sense. Jesus died into the arms of the One who sent him; he died into his resurrection.

The resurrection happens on Calvary. The two go together. The curtain was rent; a whole new reality burst forth. We must sit on Calvary a while to see this. The passerby will miss it. Calvary tells us that the Reign of God is most dramatically revealed in suffering. The Passion is a story of love. I am invited to join my passion to his.[1]

Suggestions:
  i. What struck you in this contemplation? How were you moved? Apply this to your life as seems fruitful.
  ii. Use the Consciousness Examen in ways appropriate to the Passion.
  iii. You do not need to cover everything in the Passion of Jesus. Stay with him where you find him. Focus on what he is experiencing, and then focus on what you are experiencing.
  iv. Jot down what impacted you most in your prayer.

* * * * * * * * * *

More than ever I find myself in the hands of God.
This is what I have wanted all my life from my youth.
But now there is a difference:
the initiative is entirely with God.
It is indeed a profound spiritual experience
to know and feel myself so totally in God's hands.[2]

---

[1] From a presentation by George A. Aschenbrenner, S.J., at Gonzaga University, Spokane, Washington, spring, 1983.

[2] Pedro Arrupe, S.J., cited in Harter, *Hearts on Fire,* p. 66.

THE FOURTH EXERCISE: JESUS WALKS TO THE PLACE OF HIS EXECUTION

> *. . . so that those who live might live no longer for themselves, but for him . . . .*

In the face of suffering that I cannot change, in the face of death itself, I confront the limits of my own power, even the seeming limits of the strength that comes from God . . . I become aware that I am in the presence of a loving and forgiving God . . . I offer to God this time of prayer and open my heart to all it holds.

The Scene:

I watch Jesus facing death. I hear the jeers and feel the hatred.

Grace:

I ask for what I desire: deep love and compassion for Jesus, to stay with my dying friend.

Prayer:

i. Mark 15:22-32. "Then they crucified him . . . It was about nine in the morning when they crucified him." I decide to . . . .

  ii. John 19:25-27. "Near the cross of Jesus there stood his mother . . . 'Woman, there is your son . . . There is your mother.'"

  iii. Luke 23:44-47. "Jesus uttered a loud cry . . . he expired." Do I have something to say to Jesus and his mother?

  iv. Matthew 27:57-61. ". . . And laid it in his own tomb. . . Mary Magdalene and the other Mary remained sitting there, facing the tomb." I reach out to them.

Closing:

With the dying Jesus, with Mary, John, and the others, I enter into the moment of death. Sometimes in silence is the most complete exchange. My heart opens.

Reflections:

More is said about feelings in the Third Week than in any of the other Weeks. There are the feelings of compassion, love, sorrow, grief, heart-brokenness, deep suffering, pain, affliction, confusion, sadness, lamentation . . . . Whose feelings? Jesus's feelings. This is not about getting into our own feelings; this is about getting into his. Throughout this Week, the focus continues to be on him.

Feelings of dryness and emptiness, and distractions as well, flock in during this time. This is a sharing in Jesus's Passion experience for which we have been praying during this Week. Simply let them come and return to the contemplation of Jesus. This becomes more possible the more we realize that these are Jesus's feelings we are experiencing. This is a privileged time. Stay with him. The prayer is, "I just want to be with you."

Suggestions:

i. Pray the stations of the cross.

ii. Talk with Mary about your experience of Jesus's Passion.

iii. Call to mind the people you know—individuals or groups—who are living the way of the cross today.

iv. Listen to music appropriate to this Week, such as Pergolesi's *Stabat Mater* ("Mother Standing").

THE FIFTH EXERCISE: BEING WITH JESUS IN HIS ENTIRE PASSION

. . . who for their sakes died . . . .

After someone close to me dies, I may have the Holy Saturday experience. I stay with family or friends. We sit together and go over and over the details of the death. We remember and tell what the one we love was like, things the person did. We wait . . . I become aware that I am in the presence of a loving and sustaining God . . . I offer to God this time of prayer and open my heart to what will be.

The Scene:
I picture Jesus moving through the Last Supper to his burial.

Grace:
I ask for what I desire: to be with the truth that Jesus really died out of love for my sake.

Prayer:
i. The Passion Story. Reading one of the Gospel accounts of Jesus's Passion, I let those in the story tell me their experience . . . .

ii. The Passion Story Today. I read the passion in the daily newspaper, or watch television with the heart of a mourner . . . .

iii. Luke 23:56. "Then they went home to prepare spices and perfumes. They observed the sabbath as a day of rest." I spend the sabbath with Mary and those who followed Jesus to the cross . . . .

iv. Psalm 143. "For your name's sake, O Lord, preserve me; in your justice free me from distress." I wait . . . .

Closing:

I talk with Mary about her son Jesus, or with one of the others, or perhaps with all of them, as they remember. We talk . . . .

Reflections:

The prayer of the Third Week more and more becomes that of simple presence. It is more passive, more of a resting in the mystery. This is the core of presence. It is the prayer, the experience of union between lover and beloved.

So it is that throughout the Third Week, we have come to see that it is not so much Christ who accompanies us in our struggles as it is we who accompany Christ in his.

This is gift of his Passion, that he takes our cross and places it on his; he takes our pain and makes it his. We are not alone; he is with us. He has gone through his Passion and now wants to take ours and make it his.

The grace of the Third Week is my "Yes" to union with Jesus to "be in Christ," so that my feelings are no longer mine, they are Christ's; it is no longer "I," it is "we." What is my share in Christ's Passion now? How am I living it out in my life? How is Jesus living out his Passion today—in me?

Suggestions:

   i. Let the totality of the Passion, its love and tragedy, soak deeply into your heart.

  ii. Note down which of Jesus's Passion experiences is striking you now.

 iii. Take a walk if you can and notice the phenomenon of dying in nature. Look for the Passion of Jesus in the way we humans are misusing the earth.

Stabat Mater — Mother Standing

*Standing beside the cross
on which her son hangs,
the sorrowful mother
weeps.*

*Her inmost being.
shaken, sad, grieving,
is pierced by the sword.*

*This blessed mother
of an only son
is torn by sorrow.*

*While she sees
her noble son in pain,
the gentle mother mourns.*

*What human person would
not weep
to see the mother of Christ
in such suffering?*

*Who would contemplate
Christ's mother
grieving with her son, but
could not share her
compassion?*

*She sees Jesus tortured,
beaten down with whips
for the sins of all people.*

*She sees her own dear
child
forsaken and dying, until
he breathes forth his
spirit.*

*Holy Spirit, source of love,
let me know the weight of
this sorrow.
Let me weep with our
mother.*

*Let my heart be fervent
in loving Christ my God.
Let me be pleasing to him.*

*Let the wounds of the
crucified
be fixed indelibly in my
heart,
as they are in the heart of
Mary.*

Let me carry a portion
of the pain her son
endures
so graciously for all.

Give me Mary's gift for
loving tears,
so that I will always have
compassion
for those who are being
crucified.

I desire to stand
beside the cross with Mary
and to join in her sorrow.

Strongest woman, noble
woman,
don't stand alone in bitter
sorrow.
Let me mourn with you.

I want to die with Christ,
to share his Passion.
to worship the wounded
one.

I want to know his
wounds,
to love his cross, and to

cherish
his life given for all.

Mary,
I want to stand with you,
so that
when the sword of
judgment passes
all will be vindicated.

Christ,
when it is time for me to
die,
let me come with your
mother
carrying the palm of
victory.

When my body dies,
give my soul the glory
of everlasting life with
you. Amen.

(Adapted from *Stabat Mater Dolo-rosa*, ascribed to Jacopone da Todi, O.F.M. [+1306], cited in *The Love of Christ Impels Us*, p. 155.)

TRANSITION TO THE
FOURTH GRACE (WEEK)

This final movement completes the Passover.
In joy Jesus, the Risen Christ,
appears to those he calls family,
to those he calls friends,
to console and bring life.

He draws us into surprises:
sending out women to witness,
breaking new bread with disciples,
holding out wounds to the doubter, and
stilling fears with his peace.
Rejoice in his joy. Be glad in his glory.

Rejoice as he reveals to you a new face,
as he promises to be with you
in the midst of the people,
as he shows you God in all things
sharing mutual love, and
as he sends us together

into the world
into creation
into the cosmos,
where all is made new, and
comes to fullness of life
in Christ.
Alleluia![3]

---

[3] Adapted from *The Love of Christ Impels Us,* p. 165.

PART FIVE

THE FOURTH GRACE (FOURTH WEEK): SHARING IN JESUS'S RISEN LIFE

THE FIRST EXERCISE: MARY . . . PEACE!

> *Because of this we no longer look on anyone*
> *in terms of mere human judgment . . . .*

The cause of my joy is being alive, the sense of the resurrected life, and the joy I see in other people in their resurrection experiences. The glory is a little harder to see. I do see it in the life experiences of healing and coming to know Jesus . . . I quiet myself and relax in the presence of God . . . aware of God's presence, I reverently offer this time.

The Scene: Jesus suddenly appears to his Mother, Mary, and to his disciples.

Grace:
I ask for what I desire: to rejoice and be intensely glad because of the great glory and joy of Christ who is risen.

Prayer:
  - i. Jesus visits Mary. In my imagination I go to where Jesus visits his mother. I experience every detail as he comes.

  - ii. Matthew 28:1-10. "Suddenly . . . Jesus stood before them and said, 'Peace! . . . Go and carry the news.' The women go out and proclaim the good news . . . ."

  - iii. John 20:1-18. "Presently Simon Peter came along behind him and entered the tomb . . . 'Mary!' 'Rabboni!' " Do I fail to recognize Jesus?

  - iv. People. With the people I met in the Passion, the people who were suffering, the people I meet today, I am surprised by the news that he is risen . . . .

Closing:
  I enter into conversation with Mary, with Jesus, with the people, as seems best.

Reflections:

Jesus's Passion and Resurrection are a single unit; they are but two aspects of the same experience. There is one continuous contemplation throughout both the Third and Fourth Weeks without a break.

What this says is that Jesus's resurrection happened on Calvary, his resurrection fulfilled Calvary. His suffering and death issued forth into his risen life. Separating the two leads to a disconnection of suffering from life, not only in Jesus's life but in my own. If I see only his Passion and death, I see only failure and despair, both in him and in me.

Seeing, however, the intrinsic connection between his death and resurrection reveals to me that life is always present even in the deepest sorrow and pain. Jesus's death-resurrection experience is the ultimate commentary on the problem of evil.

As Jesus told us:

> I tell you truly: you will weep and mourn while the world rejoices; you will grieve for a time, but your grief will be turned into joy . . . you are sad for a time, but I shall see you again; then your hearts will rejoice with a joy no one can take from you [John 16:20-22].

Suggestions:

    i. Select environments that reinforce your experience of Jesus's love and joy, such as making rooms colorful and bright, having pleasant thoughts and conversations, listening to beautiful music, watching the sun rise or set . . . .

    ii. Recall upon arising and frequently during the day the mystery of Jesus's resurrection to his Father. Offer acts of praise and thanksgiving to God.

    iii. Pray repeatedly for this grace of the Resurrection.

You sanctify
whatever
you are grateful for.[1]

---

[1] Anthony de Mello, S.J., cited in Harter, *Hearts on Fire,* p. 79.

THE SECOND EXERCISE:
PEACE! . . . EMMAUS

If at one time we so regarded Christ,
we no longer know him by this standard . . . .

The experience of having come through pain and
darkness into new wholeness, light, and life is an experience of victory which Jesus shares with us in the events
of our lives . . . I relax in the presence of God . . . aware
of God's awareness of me, I open my heart in reverent
joy.

The Scene:

Jesus is suddenly standing there—before us. "Peace!" He
looks so different now. The disciples stare.

Grace:

I ask for what I desire: to be filled with joy and gladness
because the risen Jesus is joyful and glorious.

Prayer:

i. John 20:19-23. "Jesus came and stood before them. 'Peace
be with you,' he said . . . at the sight of the Lord the
disciples rejoiced." Jesus goes behind the locked doors
to breathe peace on his disciples . . . .

ii. Luke 24:13-35. "Emmaus . . . 'We were hoping' . . . 'Were not our hearts burning inside us?'" Finally, when their eyes were opened, Jesus vanished from their sight. . . .

iii. John 20:24-29. "'My Lord and my God!'" Jesus stands before me and . . . .

iv. Jesus's Mystical Body. I feel invited by Jesus to see that his body, which is so wounded today, is also his risen body . . . .

Closing:

As the situation suggests, I listen and speak my heart.

Reflections:

Ignatius expects that those who have received in some measure the grace of union with Jesus in his suffering, both personal and in his mystical body, will begin to desire the experience of Jesus's joy in his resurrection. It may be that in actual fact there is no such experience. There may be only a kind of emptiness devoid of the kinds of feelings one might expect at Jesus's resurrection.

It can take time to move into this experience of joy. This is actually the work of a lifetime. The Exercises are not a closed-circuited experience, ending when they are completed. They are open-ended, becoming a way of life.

If the joy that I do feel today is truly Jesus's joy, then I will not fear losing it. It will be in him and will always be there. I am not responsible for keeping it alive. Fear of losing it and wanting to "bottle it up" so that I can drink from it whenever I want, however, is an indication that the joy I want is my own.

The kind of joy prayed for here is not necessarily a powerfully moving and uplifting experience. It may be a calmer kind of joy—one of approval of this mystery, of accepting it, of identifying with it, of living it. As is true throughout the Exercises, experiencing the joy of the risen Christ is the work of God. It is grace. We are invited into this experience; it is a gift of God to be prayed for.

Suggestions:

   i. Omit any form of penance during this Week, rejoicing instead in the fullness of life.
   ii. What is striking you in your prayer? How are you being moved? Apply it to yourself in a way that seems fruitful.
   iii. Look to see the risen Jesus in your life.

Psalm 19

The heavens bespeak the glory of God.
The firmament ablaze, a text of his works.
Dawn whispers to sunset;
Dark to dark the word passes: glory, glory.
All in a great silence,
no tongue clamor—
yet the web of the world trembles
conscious, as of great winds passing.
The bridegroom's tent is raised;
a cry goes up: "He comes!" A radiant sun
rejoicing, presiding, his wedding day.
From end to end of the universe his progress.
No creature, no least being but catches fire from him.[2]

---

[2] Daniel Berrigan, S.J., cited in Harter, *Hearts on Fire*, p.77.

The Third Exercise:
Jesus at the Seashore

> *This means that if anyone is in Christ,*
> *(s)he is a new creation . . . .*

Rising early in the morning, I may want to go walking or wait in a special place where I can be with the world as we experience the dawn breaking, the light, new life... I remember that I am in the presence of our provident God . . . aware of God's goodness and love, I give all my attention in prayer.

The Scene:
    I watch Jesus come to his disciples to feed them and encourage them.

Grace:
    I ask for what I desire: to be glad and rejoice intensely because of the great joy and glory of Christ our Lord.

Prayer:
    i. John 21:1-14. "Just after daybreak Jesus was standing on the shore . . . He said to them, 'Children, have you caught anything to eat?'" I tell Jesus what I hunger for, what I yearn for . . . .

ii. John 21:15-23. "'Simon, son of John, do you love me?... Simon, son of John, do you love me? . . . Simon, son of John, do you love me?'" I say to him, "Lord, you know everything. You know well that I love you." Jesus says to me . . . .

iii. Psalm 145. "The Lord lifts up all who are falling and raises up all who are bowed down . . . the Lord is near to all who call upon him." Gathered as believers in the risen Christ, we who have seen him pray our praise....

iv. 2 Corinthians 5:13-21. "We no longer look on anyone in terms of mere human judgment. If at one time we so regarded Christ, we no longer know him by this standard." Remembering all that has happened, we proclaim that we believe and live . . . .

Closing:
With freedom to be who I am, I express what is in my heart.

Reflections:
The grace of the Fourth Week may not be easily experienced. This alerts us to the fact that it is a gift freely given in God's own mysterious time, and also to the realization that there may be on our part resistance to it. This is paradoxical. What we desire we often resist. What makes it so difficult for the friends of Jesus to receive the joy of his resurrection?

The Emmaus story offers a clue. Jesus tells his disciples, "Did not the Messiah have to undergo all this so as to enter into his glory?" Jesus's resurrection did not undo his passion; it did not restore his life back to the way it was before his arrest. His passion and death remain; he is who he is because of them. What the resurrection tells us is that it is only through the struggles of death that we attain the joy of the resurrection. It is difficult to face the truth that we have to undergo them so as to enter into our glory.

The stories of Jesus's appearances seem to confirm this. There is a continual pattern of Jesus's appearing to his disciples, and then disappearing. He doesn't depart—he disappears. He seems to be saying to us that this is the way it will be for you in your lives. Jesus seems sometimes to be close to us and then at other times to be distant. The truth, of course, is that he is always close, even—and perhaps especially—when it seems that he is not.

The message is that we need not doubt the resurrection. Its gift is that everything becomes part of life, even death. The grace of the Fourth Week empowers us to live our resurrection continually, even in our passions and death.

Suggestions:

   i. Look for the experience of new risings in your own life.

   ii. Let your prayer grow more and more into union with the risen Jesus who is with you here and now.

   iii. Pray over your experience of Jesus risen when sharing in another's pain, even in a loved one's death.

   iv. Go back to what strikes you in your prayer.

> *Love consists in sharing*
> *what one has and what one is*
> *with those one loves.*
> *Love ought to show itself in deed*
> *more than in words.*[3]

---

[3] St. Ignatius of Loyola, cited in Harter, *Hearts on Fire,* p. 77.

THE FOURTH EXERCISE:
FEED MY SHEEP! . . . PENTECOST

He will wipe away all tears;
there will be no more death,
and no more mourning or sadness . . . .

Often I feel joy in the fulfillment that takes place in the life of Jesus. The resurrection was a big step, but not the final fulfillment. We now enter the stage of becoming what God desires for us: being like God. The creation story comes full circle, only now we actively share in the saving action of God in this world . . . I remember that I am in the presence of our saving God . . . aware of God's goodness and love, I give all my attention to prayer in joyful hope.

The Scene:
   I watch Jesus continuing to move about, teaching and encouraging his disciples. His manner is different now.

Grace:
   I ask for what I desire: to be glad and rejoice intensely because of the great joy and glory of the risen Jesus and to pray for the grace to be like him in my own time.

Prayer:

    i. John 21:15-19. "'Feed my sheep.'" Jesus is indicating to me how I am to glorify God . . . .

    ii. John 14:12. "'The one who has faith in me will do the works I do, and greater far than these.'" I . . . .

    iii. John 15:16. "'It was not you who chose me; it was I who chose you to go forth and bear fruit.'" I ponder the fruit I am to bear . . . .

    iv. Acts 2:1-13. "There came a noise like a strong, driving wind . . . tongues as of fire appeared . . . all were filled with the Holy Spirit." The Spirit is prompting me . . . .

Closing:

I wait and listen. I ask questions and respond to what I hear.

Reflections:

Many of Jesus's resurrection appearances stress his forming the Church: strengthening Peter to be the rock, the community experience of the risen Jesus, the experience of him by the faith community, the primacy of Peter, the universal mission of the Church to proclaim the Good News, the empowerment of the disciples, and so on.

The grace of the Fourth Week opens us to a realistic faith in and love of this community of faith, the Church. The word "realistic" is operative here. It suggests that this Church is very imperfect and is itself in need of salvation. Like ourselves, it too is darkened by selfishness and pride and all too often a source of hurt and injury.

The impulse to leave it because of its faults is a temptation of the First Week—the attempt to separate us from the living body of Christ today. It would not be far-fetched to imagine Jesus at times having felt the urge to abandon his disciples. Their story contains the same ambitions, factionalism, and even injustices as does the story of the Church from that time on. Jesus, however, did not give up on them. He continued to talk to them, work with them, and pray for them to view him and his work through his Spirit. This did not happen for them until the time of Pentecost, after he was gone. This is the grace of the Fourth Week that we seek: to work with and pray for this Church, for its salvation and for ours.

Suggestions:

    i. Look for the spirit of risen Jesus in the Church as you know it.

    ii. Pray continually that the Church, like yourself, will be filled with the grace of the risen Jesus.

CONTEMPLATION TO ATTAIN
LOVE OF GOD

I visualize myself within creation . . . within the body
of Christ . . . within the Communion of Saints . . . and
I celebrate our loving interdependence . . . I become
aware of the presence of God who is love, and aware that
God is lovingly aware of me.

The Scene:
I use my fantasy. I imagine that I am standing in the presence of God and amid all the blessed. They smile at me
and   seem to recommend me to God.

Grace:
I ask for what I desire: an inner knowledge of having been
so blessed by God's love that I will be entirely grateful
and impelled to love and serve God in all things.

Prayer:
i. I recall *all the gifts and blessings* with which God has
been so good to me . . . creating me . . . redeeming
me. I stay with these memories, letting myself feel how
much God has done . . . how many treasures God
shares . . . how much more God desires to give . . . I
want to offer God all that I have, and myself as well
. . . giving myself in love . . . the gift is the liberality
of God . . . I want to return all creation back to God
. . . I make my offering saying, with my whole mind
and heart, the prayer on page 117 (below), *Take, Lord,
and Receive.*

ii. I see how *God dwells* in these gifts and blessings . . . in
creation giving being to minerals, life to plants,
sensation to animals, understanding to human beings...
I sense this reality in me—God giving me being . . .
life . . . sensation . . . understanding. I am the image
of God. I remain present, until it seems right to return
God's love . . . all that I have, and myself as well. . .
giving myself in love. This is the gift of intimacy . . .
I make my offering saying, with my whole heart, the
prayer *Take, Lord, and Receive.*

iii. I perceive how *God labors in these gifts* . . . laboring for
me in all created things all over the earth. God truly
works in the universe . . . God's energy and power
being . . . sustaining . . . in things that are growing,
sensing. I enter into God's labor . . . I want to return
God's love . . . all that I do, and myself as well . . .
giving myself in love. This is the gift of union. I make
my offering saying, with my whole mind and heart, the
prayer *Take, Lord, and Receive.*

iv. I reflect on how *everything descends from above* and is
a radiance, a participation of God . . . my power, a
radiance of infinite power . . . my justice, a radiance
of perfect justice . . . my goodness . . . my compassion
. . . of God . . . like rays from the sun . . . like water
from a fountain. I rest in God's immense outpouring
of love. I want to return God's love . . . all that I have,
and myself as well . . . giving myself . . . this is the
gift of peace. I make my offering saying, with my
whole heart, the prayer, *Take, Lord, and Receive.*

Closing:

In whatever way I am moved by God's Spirit of love, I pray the prayer below with my whole mind and heart.

> *Take, Lord, and receive*
> *all my liberty,*
> *my memory, my understanding,*
> *my entire will.*
> *All that I have and possess*
> *you have given to me.*
> *To you, Christ Jesus, I return it.*
> *Everything is yours.*
> *Dispose of it*
> *according to your holy will.*
> *Give me only your love*
> *and your grace.*
> *That is enough for me.*[4]

Reflections:

The *Contemplation for Attaining Love* comes at the end of the Spiritual Exercises. Ignatius uses the lover/beloved language. It is the language of communion. It speaks of God's passionate love calling me to respond by loving and serving God in all things.

This contemplation has had a number of interpretations. One is that it is a progressive summary of the whole of the Spiritual Exercises. In this case, the first point recalls God's creating and redeeming creation and loving us just as we are. The second point recalls God's living in a special way in creation for thirty-three years in Jesus. The third point recalls God's laboring in all

---

[4] Cf. *Spiritual Exercises,* n. 234.

creation, seen especially in the Passion of Jesus. The fourth point recalls God as the source of all gifts, seen especially in the resurrection of Jesus.

A second interpretation is that the contemplation can be experienced as the "Consciousness Examen" in the following way:

- Foundation: "You are so good to us, God. Thank you."
- First Week: "We need you, God. Help us."
- Second Week: "We want to know and love you, Jesus."
- Third Week: "We will stay with you in your suffering."
- Fourth Week: "We rejoice with you, Christ. Stay with us."

A third interpretation is that this contemplation is the culmination and fruit of the Spiritual Exercises in that they lead to the discovery of one's own spirituality, the experience of one's relationship with the mystery of God. In this interpretation:

- The first point of the contemplation presents God as "parent, giver, provider, abundant bestower." This perception lends itself to trusting in and abandoning oneself to God.
- The second point describes God as "abiding in, indwelling in, all things." This view is most naturally experienced in the desire for intimacy with God.
- The third point highlights God as "creating, serving, in action, moving all to the final end." This way of looking at God leads a person to work with the Spirit in achieving God's final reign.

- The fourth point sees God as "source of all, the power in all, the energy within." God is here prayed to as the source of all inspirations and guidance in the world.[5]

However one views the "Contemplation to Attain the Love of God," its grace is to ask for the deep knowledge of the many blessings received, so that, filled with gratitude for them, I may love and serve God in all things.

Suggestions:

i. Pray *To a God Whose Name Is Love*, on page 120.

ii. Compose your own offering prayer according to how you have been graced by God during these Exercises.

iii. Find a way of pulling together and celebrating your spiritual growth throughout this experience. What began as a set of Ignatius's Spiritual Exercises has now become the experience of your own Spiritual Exercises. Develop a ritual of closing according to how your spirit was touched.

iv. Reflect on what way you live the mystery of God in your life.

---

[5] Stephen V. Sundborg, S.J., presentation at Loyola Retreat House (Portland, Oregon, summer 1994).

TO A GOD WHOSE NAME IS LOVE

(i) What return can I make to you, Love?
for all your goodness to me?
I will take up the cup of sharing;
I will bless your bountiful name.
I will do what I vowed to you, Love,
in the presence of all creation.

(ii) What return can I make to you, Love?
for always dwelling in me?
I will take up the cup of welcome;
I will image your indwelling name.
I will do what I vowed to you, Love,
in the body of all creation.

(iii) What return can I make to you, Love?
for all your labor for me?
I will offer the gift of my life;
I will live for your name.
I will do what I vowed to you, Love,
by my work for all creation.

(iv) What return can I make to you, Love?
for your infinite love filling me?
I will love with the love of creating;
I will make new your name.
I will fulfill what I vowed to you, Love,
in completing your gift of creation.[6]

---

[6] From *The Love of Christ Impels Us*, p. 189.

APPENDICES

- THE CONSCIOUSNESS EXAMEN

- MAKING MORAL CHOICES:
DISCERNMENT IN THE FIRST WEEK

- CHOOSING TO FOLLOW CHRIST:
DISCERNMENT IN THE SECOND WEEK

- TIMES FOR MAKING A DECISION

- SEEKING CONFIRMATION FOR A DECISION

- LIVING OUT THE SPIRITUAL EXERCISES

- THE LIFE OF SAINT IGNATIUS

- BIBLIOGRAPHY

- ACKNOWLEDGEMENTS

THE CONSCIOUSNESS EXAMEN

The Consciousness Examen is a prayer of discernment. The following is one model.

1. "Thank you." God loves us and reaches out to us in love. I recognize this love in what I have received today—in people, events, nature, graces. I respond in gratitude.

2. "Help me." I feel inadequate in the face of such love. I feel insensitive and ungrateful. I ask God's Spirit to help me see and respond to God's action in me.

3. "I do love you." I see with the Spirit's help how Christ has been in my life.

4. "I am sorry." I am aware that I failed to see and respond to God in me. I turn to God like the prodigal child, confident that I will be received in love. God is abundantly welcoming to me.

5. "Be with me." Through Spirit, I ask to be with Christ and to respond full-heartedly in the future. I express my hope in love.[1]

---

[1] John Carroll Futrell, S.J., and Marian Cowan, C.S.J., *The Spiritual Exercises of St. Ignatius of Loyola: A Handbook for Directors* (New York: LeJacq Publishing, 1982), p. 35.

The Consciousness Examen is not about good or bad actions, but about how God is moving me. Its focus is not on me; it is on God <u>in</u> me and how I respond to God's loving initiative. The Examen makes us more aware of our inner movements and of which are Spirit-inspired. The goal of the Examen is to develop a discerning heart throughout all of life. Finding God in all things is what life is all about. My life is no longer an "I"; it is a "we."

MAKING MORAL CHOICES:
DISCERNMENT OF SPIRITS
DURING THE FIRST GRACE (WEEK)

When moving away from behavior that is compulsive and out of accord with God, the main concern is self-understanding and radical separation from sin. This involves a struggle between feelings of self-gratification or self-diminishment and the desire to be with God. The following are paraphrases of Ignatius's rules for the discernment of spirits for the First Week.

A. The struggle between God's touch (good spirits) and resistance to it (evil spirits):
   1. If you are caught in a sinful pattern, the evil spirit will reinforce what is attractive. The good spirit, however, will appeal to your conscience, and you will feel remorse.
   2. If you are becoming free, the opposite happens. An evil spirit will present obstacles to what is good, leading to sadness and discouragement.

B. The experience of spiritual consolation and of spiritual desolation:
   3. Spiritual consolation is the inner experience of the love of God in which everything seems loveable only in relation to God. It may be the experience of tears for God's love or for sorrow for sin. It is every increase of faith, hope, and love, and of all inner joy that comes from union with God. It brings quiet and peace in God's presence.
   4. Spiritual desolation is inner darkness, turmoil, and separation from self and from God. It is an experience of disturbance and temptation leading to fear, hopeless-

ness, lack of self-respect, or feelings of laziness, luke-warmness, sadness.

C. *Acting against feelings of desolation:*

5. When in desolation, do not change what you decided when in consolation. Doing so is the counsel of an evil spirit.

6. Change your behavior by praying more and doing penance.

D. *Acting against thoughts arising from desolation:*

7. Remember when feeling lost and alone in temptation that God is always with you and will always give you what you need.

8. Be patient, no matter how upset you feel. You will again be consoled.

9. Possible reasons for desolation:

a. You have been lukewarm, lazy, or neglectful in your spiritual exercises, so your inner self is warning you.

b. You are being given an opportunity to recognize how much you are devoted to God and how much you are just giving in to pleasant feelings.

c. You may be receiving a gift of knowing that you cannot control feelings and thoughts, that you do not possess anything on your own, that you cannot take pride in your spiritual growth since all is gift from God.

E. *Growth in times of consolation:*

10. When you experience consolation, remember that you will also feel desolation in the future and gather strength for that time.

11. When you experience consolation, be humble and

grateful, thinking how little you can do without such grace; and when you experience desolation think that God will strengthen you with the grace you need.

F. Acting against the bad spirits which foster desolation.
   12. Stand firm. Bad spirits attack when you show fear and flee when you demonstrate courage.
   13. Be open with a trustworthy person about what you are experiencing, since evil spirits flourish in secrecy and disappear in openness.
   14. Do all you can to gain self-knowledge of your strengths and weaknesses, knowing that bad spirits attack where you are weakest.[2]

It is important not to confuse spiritual consolation and desolation with surface feelings. One can experience fear and anxiety and still be in consolation. Profound well-being and harmony with God and self are deeper than surface feelings. So, for example, relief at coming to a decision may not be the consolation of confirmation; it may be the wrong decision. Fear at confronting abusive behavior can co-exist with consolation, since the respect of self is honored more than the ease of not confronting the abuser.

---

[2] Taken from *The Love of Christ Impels Us,* p. 230. Cf. Spiritual Exercises, nn. 313-327.

CHOOSING TO FOLLOW CHRIST:
DISCERNMENT OF SPIRITS
DURING THE SECOND GRACE (WEEK)

The concern when wanting to commit to Jesus is to distinguish between what only appears to lead to him from what truly does. The alternating movements are feelings that appear good but lead away from good, and feelings that do lead towards the true good.

Consolation from God, and consolation from an evil spirit—discerning how to respond:

1. God's spirit is at work when what is moving you gives real gladness and spiritual joy, taking away all sadness and disturbance. The evil spirit does the opposite. It takes away spiritual gladness and peace by bringing up doubts, anxiety, and false ways of thinking.

2. Consolation is from God when there has been no previous occurrence causing it, because it is God's prerogative to draw the soul into love for the divinity.

3. Consolation from the good spirit moves you from the good to the better. Consolation from an evil spirit draws you away from the good to what is less good.

4. The evil spirit appears to be moving you toward good, but leads you away from good. It inspires good and holy intentions, but little by little it deceives in hidden ways.

5. Watch where movements lead. If they begin, continue, and end in good, they are the work of the good spirit.

If, however, they end in something bad, distract from the good intended, lead to something less than what was originally intended, or weaken, disturb, or cause loss of peace, they are the work of the evil spirit.

6. When the work of the evil spirit is recognized, review how thoughts which seemed good in the beginning gradually moved you away from joy and peace and brought you toward what is not good. This will help you recognize the evil spirit at work and recognize how to avoid getting caught in the same pattern again.

7. When going from good to better, the good spirit touches you in a delicate, gentle, light way—light a drop of water entering a sponge. The evil spirit, however, touches you in a harsh, noisy, disquieting way—like a drop of water falling on stone. When going from bad to worse, the opposite is true. The reason is that a spirit either finds itself at home with your inner disposition and therefore comes in quietly, or it is not at home and makes a lot of noise forcing itself in.

8. When an instance of consolation has no previous cause, you can trust that it is of God. In the warm afterglow that follows, however, your habits, thoughts, and judgments, or other spirits—good or evil—may influence opinions and decisions that are not from God. They need to be examined well before being put into action.[3]

---

[3] *Ibid.,* p. 234. See Spiritual Exercises, nn. 328-336.

Times for Making a Decision

I soon become aware while doing the Exercises that there are some decisions that need to be made. They may be small choices, or they may be life-orienting. Ignatius describes three times when a person may make a correct and good decision regarding his or her life.

A. *First time: decision without hesitation*

Sometimes I make a decision without having to work at it. It just comes. I simply know what is God's inspiration, and I will follow up on it. I may feel enthusiasm, or I may proceed in quiet peace; but I act without hesitation.

B. *Second time: decision through discernment*

Often I am not sure whether or not a possibility I am considering is God-inspired. Feelings and desire pull me in different directions, and I am not able to see clearly what will lead me to life. By attending to these alternating feelings of attraction and repulsion, I can coöperate with God's grace of discernment and come to a good decision. Then joy, acceptance, creative love, and deep peace will point me to new grace-filled life.

C. *Third time: decision by faith-filled reasoning*

Sometimes I consider what God may be inviting me to do or not do without much feeling one way or another. There just are no inner affective movements. Within the spirit of faith, I consider as fully as I can the possibility I am considering, and then I make a decision in the belief that this is God-inspired. Then I seek confirmation.[4]

---

[4] *Ibid.,* p. 228. Cf. Spiritual Exercises, nn. 175-177.

SEEKING CONFIRMATION FOR A DECISION

Decision-making in the Exercises may be about something
specific in one's life. It may also be about something more
substantial, more generic, having to do with attitude and
orientation. Decisions once made need to be placed prayerfully
before God's open and generous Spirit for confirmation that the
decision made is indeed God-inspired.

Confirmation of a decision is often an afterthought, something
which is done some time after a decision has been made. But
confirmation can occur within the decision-making process
itself. The deep peace and sense of harmony with oneself, the
world, and God is sought for during the work of deciding. The
deciding is not finished until the confirmation is experienced.
One making the Exercises may have already made a tentative
decision and is now seeking confirmation within the Exercises.

LIVING OUT THE SPIRITUAL EXERCISES

And know that I am with you always,
until the end of the world . . . .

The graces of the Spiritual Exercises continue.

You have just finished the Spiritual Exercises of St. Ignatius. As you progressed through them, they gradually became your own spiritual exercises. Your personal effort and God's grace do not end here. They continue; in fact, they may be just beginning. Ignatius himself emphasized that if we do not desire a grace, that we pray to desire it. What this means is that the graces of the Exercises may not be experienced until later, perhaps much later and at the most unexpected times. They may suddenly appear without anything in particular happening, or they may appear within the middle of an experience.

What this suggests is that living out the Exercises—your spiritual exercises—is as foundational for you as formally doing them. In fact, it is very often within lived daily experiences that the graces of the Exercises are received.

Please consider the following suggestions as you look ahead.

  i. Pray through those meditations and contemplations in the Exercises to which you feel drawn.

 ii. Read through your journal, praying over those points which strike you in some way, whether positively or negatively.

iii. Seek spiritual direction regarding the work of God's Spirit within you from here on.

iv. Seek confirmation of your spiritual journey from your spiritual community.

v. Share your experience of your spiritual exercises with a trusted friend.

vi. Pray for the Spirit's guidance in your personal prayer regarding focus, frequency, when in the day, where, style of prayer, and so on.

vii. Prayerfully reflect on how your experience of these Exercises has moved you to be Christ for others.

viii. Prayerfully reflect on what in your life needs to be brought into your spiritual exercises.

ix. Prayerfully reflect on the influence that your cultural and political settings have on your way of being Christ for the world.

x. Always seek calm and deep peace in your relationship with God. Anxiety and narcissistic guilt are not of God.

ST. IGNATIUS OF LOYOLA, 1491-1556[5]

PART I

In 1491, a year before Columbus discovered the West Indies, Iñigo de Loyola was born in a Basque castle in the very country in which Don Quixote and Sancho searched for giants. Iñigo too was to become a man unafraid to dream of a kingdom. Although they were of noble blood, the Loyolas were not greatly wealthy. Like many other noblemen, Iñigo was trained to exquisite courtesy and especially to a chivalrous attention to women; but there was not much hope that the eleventh of eleven children would prosper unless he entered the Church or lived by his wits and sword.

Iñigo was a courtier, a conquistador, a musketeer. The commandments were of course unquestionable in theory, but practice was entirely another matter. Church was for times of danger or for celebration of victory, and he never prayed so hard to our Lady as before a duel. His biographer later wrote,

Though he was attached to the faith, he lived no way in conformity with it and did not avoid sin. Rather, he was much addicted to gambling and dissolute in his dealings with women, contentious and keen about using his sword.

But back-street brawling lacked the scope of his dreams, so in 1517 Iñigo joined the command of the Duke of Najera occupying Pamplona, on the border between France and the newly appropriated Spanish Navarre. The citizens of the occupied territory tolerated their new masters with fiery eyes. Their opportunity for revenge and freedom came when thousands of French troops poured through the passes of the

---

[5] The pages on the life of St. Ignatius which follow are excerpted and adapted from William J. O'Malley, S.J., *The Fifth Week* (Chicago: Loyola Press, 1976), pp. 9-27 *passim*, and are cited with permission of Loyola Press.

Pyrenees to liberate them. Rejoicing villages greeted the French with open gates and the Council of Pamplona practically gave them the keys of the city. With more prudence than courage, the commander of the Pamplona garrison saw which way the wind was blowing and deserted. The hot-headed Iñigo was furious and rallied around him the men willing to defend at least the citadel in the center of town. When the captains actually saw twelve thousand men and thirty cannon drawn up against the city, it took all of Iñigo's badgering and shaming to stiffen their backs to salvage, if not Pamplona, at least their honor.

The French offered terms of surrender. Iñigo persuaded the governor not to accept them. Because no priest was present, Iñigo, following a custom of the Middle Ages, confessed his sins to a comrade. Then he took his post on the breastworks. For six hours the French pounded the citadel, and finally part of the wall crumbled and the infantry prepared to pour in. In the breach stood Iñigo, sword drawn to meet the attack. And there he fell, his right leg shattered by a shell. Surrender of the garrison followed immediately. . . . The French treated their wounded prisoner with that delicate courtesy which prompted them to carry him in a litter to Loyola, but which could never be a substitute for surgical competence, so distressingly wanting when they tried to set his broken leg. At Loyola the doctors of Azpeitia tried to remedy the mistakes of the French. It was an agonizing experience, and years later Ignatius spoke of it as "butchery." He failed to rally after the operation, became more and more weak, received the last sacraments, and almost died. Then came a turn for the better and his strength gradually returned. However, the doctors had left his leg in a condition intolerable to a man who still would be the gallant courtier and soldier. The sections of the broken bone did not mesh smoothly and evenly, one piece actually resting astride another. This caused a notable protrusion and made the leg shorter than the other. Ignatius could not abide this deformity and insisted on another operation even though it entailed agony of the worst kind.[6]

He bore it all in silence, he says, not for the love of God, nor to do penance for his sins, but in order to wear again the handsome tight-fitting boots which caught ladies' eyes.

As Iñigo lay at Loyola recovering from this second operation, he whiled away the time with daydreams of his lady, a woman he said was "more than a countess or duchess." Whether she was merely a creature of hope and imagination or one of the high Spanish nobility (Princess Catherine, younger sister of Emperor Charles V has been suggested) he doesn't say; but he spent hours and hours daydreaming of what he would say to her, of the glorious deeds he would offer her as her knight.

As the days dragged by, Iñigo asked for books of chivalry to feed his dreams, but all the castle could offer were *The Life of Christ* and *The Lives of the Saints*, thin fare for one who fed on battles and jousts and similar excitement. So he reluctantly picked up the two books. He was moving into his first retreat.

Slowly turning the pages, Iñigo found himself daydreaming about the lives of Jesus and the saints in the same way he had dreamed away the hours with his princess. His curiosity was caught by the fact that the book of saints called these men "the Knights of God dedicated to the eternal prince, Jesus Christ." They were persons who drew from the gospels the courage to battle an evil more subtle than guns. He imagined himself as Dominic preaching and Francis begging; he saw himself walking the hills with Jesus. And his daydreams grew overwhelming.

---

[6] William V. Bangert, S.J., *A History of the Society of Jesus* (Saint Louis: Institute of Jesuit Sources, 1986), p. 5.

But then it began to fade. Gradually these thoughts yielded to the old familiar glories in the gunsmoke, sabres flashing, wounds borne proudly for the glory of the king. Then back again to the yearning for a more elusive glory, binding wounds, serving the poor, following a king from beyond time. As he watched the swing of thoughts back and forth, he came to see that his romantic daydreams left him empty and dry, while his dreams of laboring with Christ gave him a profound joy and peace. He began to suspect that the peace and joy he felt were a touchstone of the truth, a call which said more and more certainly that the glorious world of the court and camp was less real and less permanent than the sacrificial world of the cross. He had come to that moment when a person stands helplessly before the Lord and asks, "All right! What do you want me to do?"

Then one night as he lay awake, he, who to the end of his life distrusted extraordinary phenomena, beheld Mary holding the child Jesus. It was a presence which threw his past, especially his sexual self-indulgence, into a light from which there was no hiding. It was the undeniable moment:

> Thus from that hour until August 1553 when this was written, he never gave the slightest consent to the things of the flesh. For this reason it may be considered the work of God, although he did not dare to claim it nor said more than to affirm the above.[7]

He was a knight who had found his Lady and his King.

Ignatius was a great-souled, ambitious person, too big to live the comfortable, quiet life of a kindly Christian. Once he chose a road, he went down it like a hurricane. Before the end of his convalescence, he had resolved to give up everything, and to go

---

[7] Ignatius of Loyola, *A Pilgrim's Testament: The Memoirs of Saint Ignatius of Loyola*, tr. Parmananda Divarkar, S.J. (Saint Louis: Institute of Jesuit Sources, 1995), p. 39.

to the Holy Land. As sinner or saint, he could never be content to go half way.

As he traveled to the port of Barcelona, he stopped at the Benedictine shrine perched high in the mountains of Montserrat. He made a general confession in writing; it lasted three days.[8] On March 24, 1522, with his past behind him, he began a completely new life. He gave his mule to the monastery, exchanged clothes with a beggar, hung his sword and dagger on the grill in our Lady's chapel, and kept vigil there through the night in preparation for the new kind of battle he knew he was about to begin.

There was much Ignatius had to discover about himself and about the new life he had been drawn into; and so, postponing his pilgrimage to the Holy Land, he remained at the little town of Manresa, near Montserrat, to wrestle with himself and with God. There he resolved to rival even the saints in his rejection of his past worldliness. Because he had been so fastidious about his appearance, he now tramped through the village begging his food, body unwashed, hair and nails uncut, followed by a gaggle of urchins yelling after him, "Old bag, old bag!" He helped the sick in the hospitals, attended daily Mass, and spent seven hours a day in prayer, on his knees.

Much later in his life, he says in his autobiography,

God treated him at this time just as a schoolmaster treats a child whom he is teaching. Whether this was because of his lack of education and of brains, or because he had no one to teach him. . . .[9]

But his Schoolmaster surely allowed him to make almost every possible mistake before correcting him.

His penances were merciless. At first to copy the saints and then to prove his good will to God, he beat himself with a rope,

---

[8] *Ibid.*, p. 24.
[9] *Ibid.*, p. 39.

fasted, slept rough and little. In the beginning it gave him great joy. It seemed so obviously the right thing to do, to teach the flesh who was in charge, to punish the instrument of his sins. It was much easier than discovering what he learned later: the slow crucifixion of unequivocal honesty about oneself. And then there were the temptations. It seemed cowardly and ungenerous to ease up on the penances. Yet pushing them further was to court vanity for being so holy. But worst of all were the voices: "How will you be able to endure this life for the seventy years you have to live?" Even in his abandonment, he was wise enough to answer, "Wretch! Can you promise me an hour of life?"[10]

It was the dark night of the soul. Prayer became bleak torment: scruples over possibly unconfessed sins ravaged him. It was a nightmare so awful that he was tempted to suicide. Still continuing his regimen of prayer and penance, he resolved that he would neither eat or drink until God came to his rescue—and all that week he put nothing in his mouth.

And the scruples continued. Then came the day of decision. He resolved at that moment once and for all that he would never again confess his past sins. And he was from that moment unconditionally free.

Then, in a way most of us cannot even imagine, the soul of Ignatius opened to share in the aliveness of God. The most incandescent of these experiences occurred while he was sitting one day on the bank of the river Cardoner. Without his seeing any vision, wave after wave of understanding enraptured him, filling him with a union of mind and will with God. It was an experience so intense that he seemed to himself to be another person, with another mind than that which was his before.

From that time onward he opened up more to people and took greater pains to make himself agreeable to them. For this

---

[10] *Ibid.*, p. 32.

reason, after he had finally collapsed from his excessive fasting and penance, he cheerfully left behind him his more rigorous self-torments, along with his outlandish clothes, his long hair, and his long nails.

THE SPIRITUAL EXERCISES

During this crucial period of his life, Ignatius began to sketch the lines of what became a little book by which others could attain the insights and freedom he had achieved without repeating his near-fatal mistakes. By the time (several years later) he had essentially completed the *Spiritual Exercises*, he envisioned a retreatant with a director working step by step through four weeks of meditations and contemplations in order to bring the retreatant to a freedom of vision where (s)he could see God's will without fear of selfishness getting in the way.

The book's basic premise, repeated over and over, is that growth in aliveness of the spirit is made only in proportion to the surrender of self-centeredness; there is only one Center. Over four weeks the retreatant ponders the purpose and fulfillment of human life and the sin which prevents it. (S)he ponders Christ living human life in its fullest, loving his brothers and sisters even to the ultimate sacrifice of himself. (S)he ponders Christ's sacrifice of himself, leading to the resurrection of a new person born free of time and space, free of selfishness and death, free to love.

THE PILGRIM

Toward the end of February, 1523, Ignatius left Manresa for the Holy Land, blissfully indifferent to the fact that he hadn't a peso to his name. God wanted him to go to Palestine, and neither bad weather nor pirates, neither Turks nor starvation was going to stop him. And they all had a try at him. He determined to stay in the Holy Land to convert the Turks; but the Franciscan superior, fearing what a newly converted fanatic could do to uneasy relations with the Moslems, vetoed his plans.

With his dreams of the Holy Land behind him, Ignatius returned to Europe and decided to study. He could already read and write—no mean achievement, since fewer than five percent of the adults at that time had training in those skills equivalent to that possessed by a seven-year-old today. But Ignatius knew no Latin, so at the age of thirty-three he went to school with small boys to study Latin for two years. After brief stays at the universities of Alcala and Salamanca, he went to the University of Paris, the most renowned in Christendom, to pursue his studies.

He completed his master's degree at age forty-three, despite his poor health from his earlier penances. He tells us in his autobiography,

> In Paris already by this time he [Ignatius always refers to himself in the third person] was quite unwell in the stomach, so that every fifteen days he had a stomach ache which lasted over an hour and gave him a fever. Once the stomach ache lasted sixteen or seventeen hours. At this time he had already finished the Arts course and studied theology for some years, and gathered the companions. His trouble kept getting worse and worse, and he could not find a cure, though many were tried.[11]

For thirty years until his death Ignatius suffered this way. After embalming his body, the doctor would note that he had personally extracted almost numberless stones of various colors found in the kidneys, the lungs, the liver, and the portal vein.

---

[11] *Ibid.*, p. 120.

THE SOCIETY OF JESUS

During these years of study Ignatius gave the Spiritual Exercises to a number of his fellow students. Eventually seven of these became unshakably committed to him. On the feast of the Assumption in 1534, they left the Latin Quarter in Paris and went to the chapel of St. Denis on Montmartre, where they took three vows of poverty, chastity, and a pilgrimage to Jerusalem. They travelled to Venice and waited to go to the Holy Land, but the wars around the Mediterranean postponed their passage. During this time they were all ordained priests and spent their time in various Italian cities preaching, hearing confessions, giving the Exercises, and sheltering and feeding victims of the plague. After they went to Rome, their reputation grew so rapidly that the pope called on them to settle disputes and take on the reform of monasteries.

The will of God regarding going to Jerusalem became evident, and they met to decide their future. They eventually decided, in 1539, after much prayer and discernment, to petition the pope to let them become a religious order different from the others of the time. Theirs would be primarily apostolic, not secluded in a monastery but out in the streets serving God by serving God's people. On September 27, 1540, they received the approval from Pope Paul III which made the Society of Jesus a reality. During the Lent of the following year, over his agonized protests, Ignatius, at age fifty, was unanimously elected the first general of the Society of Jesus.

THE GENERAL

For sixteen years Ignatius served at a desk as general. During that time, among many other things, he wrote nearly seven thousand letters, screened applicants to the Society, opened homes for orphans and reformed prostitutes, and carved out the Constitutions of the Society of Jesus.

By 1556 the sickness which had plagued Ignatius for years became worse. He had fits of shivering and fever, and he often couldn't get up for days at a time. On July 31, 1556, between six and six thirty in the morning, the "wanderer of Loyola" began his last pilgrimage.

IGNATIUS THE MAN

Ignatius is often pictured by people who know him little as a stern man of iron will and of military demeanor. Nothing could be further from the truth. He could be firm with those who could take it; and yet Da Camara, who took down the text of Ignatius's autobiography, observed, "He was always rather inclined toward love; moreover, he seemed all love, and because of that he was universally loved by all." He sometimes cried so much at Mass that he could not go on nor even talk for some time, and he was afraid that his gift of tears might cause him to lose his eyesight.

Ignatius was a man of great practical and common sense. A Jesuit had complained of having trouble with overly pious people who monopolized his time for no good reason. Through Polanco, Ignatius instructed him on how to deal charitably with such people without giving offense: in the case of someone whom there was no hope of helping, he observed, it would be useful to discourse pointedly on hell, judgment, and such things. That being done, either the person would depart and not return, or, if he did come back, the chances would good that he would feel himself touched in the Lord.

There was a bishop who had great animosity toward the Society. He refused to allow this new order in his diocese, and he excommunicated anyone who made the Spiritual Exercises.

He was known as "Bishop Cilicio" ("the hairshirt bishop") by the Jesuits. Ignatius told the Jesuits who were worried about his attitude to relax; Bishop Cilicio was an old man and the Society was young: the Society could afford to wait.

Ignatius was a man who was utterly free inside, free of preconceived ideas, free of fear, free of the opinions of others. He was amazingly able to adapt to the unforeseen and amazingly alive to the call of God from whatever quarter that call might come. He was loyal to the inspirations of "his King." The legacy of Ignatius is not a gift but a challenge: to serve God with unrelenting freedom, even from oneself.

BIBLIOGRAPHY

BOOKS

Barry, William A., S.J. *Finding God in All Things.* Notre Dame, IN.: Ave Maria Press, 1991.

Brueggemann, Walter. *The Prophetic Imagination.* Philadelphia: Fortress Press, 1983.

Callahan, William R. *Noisy Contemplation.* Hyattesville, MD: Quixote Center, 1994.

English, John, S.J. *Sharing Experiences of the Spiritual Exercises.* Guelph: Office of English Canada, 1994.

Fleming, David L., S.J. *The Spiritual Exercises of St. Ignatius: A Literal Translation and A Contemporary Reading.* St. Louis: Institute of Jesuit Sources, 1978. (Later editions of this work, from the same publisher, appear under title of *A Contemporary Reading of the Spiritual Exercises: A Companion to St. Ignatius's Text* [1980], *The Spiritual Exercises of Saint Ignatius: A Literal Translation & A Contemporary Reading* [1980, 1982, 1985, 1989, 1991], *Draw Me Into Your Friendship: A Literal Translation and a Contemporary Reading of the Spiritual Exercises* [1996].)

Futrell, John, S.J., and Cowan, Marian, C.S.J. *The Spiritual Exercises of St. Ignatius: A Handbook for Directors.* New York: LeJacq Publishing, 1982.

Harter, Michael G., S.J. *Hearts on Fire: Praying with Jesuits.* Saint Louis: Institute of Jesuit Sources, 1993.

O'Malley, William J., S.J. *The Fifth Week*. Chicago: Loyola Press, 1976.

Sisters of Providence. *The Love of Christ Impels Us: Providence Retreat in Everyday Life*. Spokane, WA: privately published, 1991.

ARTICLE

Osiek, Carolyn, R.S.C.J. "The First Week of the Spiritual Exercises and the Conversion of Saint Paul." In David L. Fleming, S.J., (ed), *Notes on the Spiritual Exercises*. Saint Louis: Review for Religious, 1983.

ACKNOWLEDGEMENTS

I am indebted to the Sisters of Providence of Spokane, Washington, for their permission to adapt the format and some of the content from their handbook on the Spiritual Exercises entitled *The Love of Christ Impels Us*. This content is seen mostly in some of the introductory paragraphs to an exercise, in some of the comments around the given scriptures, and in the poetic prayers between each grace (week).

I am indebted to Cora Lee Mack for her careful reading of the manuscript of this book and for her insightful suggestions that did so much to make the presentations (especially of the First Week) more understandable and accessible to the reader.

I also acknowledge with gratitude the permission of the director of Loyola Press, Chicago, for his permission to cite excerpts from William J. O'Malley, S.J., *The Fifth Week*, published by Loyola in 1976.

Also cited are works published by the Institute of Jesuit Sources, Saint Louis, notably William V. Bangert, S.J., *A History of the Society of Jesus* (1986), Michael G. Harter, S.J. (ed.), *Hearts on Fire: Praying with Jesuits* (1993), and Parmananda R. Divarkar, S.J. (trans.), *A Pilgrim's Testament: The Memoirs of St. Ignatius of Loyola* (1995).